1 & 2 Peter
Quick Study Commentary

By Chad Sychtysz

Published by
Spiritbuilding Publishers
9700 Ferry Road, Waynesville, Ohio 45068

1 & 2 PETER QUICK STUDY COMMENTARY
By Chad Sychtysz

ISBN: 978–1–964–80532–0

Spiritbuilding
PUBLISHERS

spiritbuilding.com

Table of Contents

Introduction to *1 Peter*

The First Epistle of Peter (*1 Peter*) is a favorite study of many Bible students. While it lacks the doctrinal content of, say, *Romans* or *Ephesians*, *1 Peter* is an excellent handbook for ideal Christian behavior, and for submission to various people and authorities. "To this day *First Peter* is one of the easiest letters in the New Testament to read, for it has never lost its winsome appeal to the human heart."[1] It is intensely practical in nature. "The chief value of First Peter is that it shows Christians how to live a redeemed life in the midst of a world contrary and hostile to them."[2] Peter shows us what it means to take up our cross and follow Christ (Mat. 16:24). "He speaks with the authority of an apostle, but with the gentleness of one who knew the power of temptation and the difficulty of steadfastness, with the humility of one who well remembered how he himself had fallen."[3]

First Peter falls into the category of "general epistles"—letters written to no one person or church, but to Christians who are "scattered throughout" the Anatolian Peninsula (modern-day Turkey) (1:1). General epistles are no less valuable to us than personal ones, and Peter's epistle carries all the same apostolic authority as Paul's epistles. Peter refers to his reading audience as "aliens" (or, "strangers")—in essence, spiritual pilgrims who are dwelling *in* the world, but, through their allegiance to Christ, are no longer *of* the world. While he names specific places where such believers reside, his instruction and ultimate intention is for all believers in every place and every age. Just as those in ancient Anatolia were "chosen" (1:1), so all Christians have been called and chosen through their having responded to Christ's gospel in obedience. The phrase "scattered throughout" (1:1) is derived from

---

1 William Barclay, *The Letters of James and Peter* (Philadelphia: Westminster Press, 1960), 164.

2 Roy E. Cogdill, *The New Testament: Book by Book* (Marion, IN: Cogdill Foundation, 1975), 156.

3 B. C. Caffin, "1 Peter," *The Pulpit Commentary*, vol. 22 (Peabody, MA: Hendrickson Publishers, no date), iv.

a single Greek word [*diaspora*] which, when capitalized, refers to the historical scattering of Jews beyond the region of Palestine and into the Roman Empire and beyond (see John 7:35 and James 1:1).[4] Thus, some think that Peter wrote only to Jewish Christians, yet the full content of his letter does not support this (consider 2:10 and 4:3, for example). By implication, *all* Christians become spiritual Jews since they are all part of "the Israel of God" (Gal. 6:16) and the "New Jerusalem" (Heb. 12:22).

Purpose and Theme: Peter's purpose in writing to Christians abroad is not merely to send greetings or offer a few words of encouragement. There is little mention of false teachers, false teaching, or false brethren—subjects which occupy a great deal of attention in Paul's writings—but an intense focus on the Christian's spiritual perspective of himself (or herself) in an ungodly world. Peter states his own purpose for writing in 5:12: to exhort and testify of the true grace of God, especially to those suffering severe trials for their faith.

> [Peter's] object seems to be, by the prospect of their heavenly portion and by Christ's example, to afford consolation to the persecuted, and prepare them for a greater approaching ordeal, and to exhort all, husbands, wives, servants, presbyters [elders], and people, to a due discharge of relative duties, so as to give no handle to the enemy to reproach Christianity, but rather to win them to it, and so to establish them in "the true grace of God wherein they stand" (1 Peter 5:12).[5]

The content of Peter's sermons in *Acts* (chapters 2–5 and 10) and that of his epistle outlines the basic belief system of what has come to be known as Christianity. This theology has five basic parts, which comprise one grand message:

---

4   Such dispersion was sometimes voluntary, as Jews moved to foreign nations to seek better (and sometimes safer) opportunities, but the primary reason was due to captivity, exile, and forced resettlement by secular authorities.

5   Robert Jamieson, Andrew Fausset, and David Brown, *Jamieson, Fausset, and Brown Commentary: Commentary Critical and Explanatory on the Whole Bible (1871)*, electronic edition (database © 2012 by WORDsearch Corp.), "Introduction"; bracketed words are mine.

- **First:** the age of fulfillment of the Old Testament (OT) prophecies has come, and the reign of the Messiah (Christ) has begun. This proclamation is God's final revelation to the world; a new (spiritual) world order or age has begun, and people are invited to join the new community of believers.
- **Second:** This new age has come through the life, death, and resurrection of Jesus Christ, who has fulfilled all the prophecies concerning Him in the OT. Thus, He and His reign are the result of God's eternal plan and divine foreknowledge (Eph. 3:11).
- **Third:** By virtue of Christ's life and resurrection, He has been exalted to the right hand of God as the holy King of the new and spiritual Israel, the church (Acts 2:33).
- **Fourth:** The Messianic reign will reach its consummation in Christ's return to bring His saints to glory, and to usher in the great day of the Lord in which all the living and dead will be judged (Heb. 9:27–28).
- **Fifth:** All these facts provide the basis for an appeal to all people to repent, and for God to offer forgiveness through the blood of His Son, and to give His Holy Spirit to those who have been born again into a new fellowship with God.[6]

The moral purity of the believer is necessary for one's participation in this grand scheme of salvation (1:13–16, 2:1–2, 2:11–12, etc.). Peter sympathizes with those who are going through difficult times, but he never gives anyone permission to be anything different than what is required of all believers. Collectively, he refers to these people as the "chosen race," "royal priesthood," "holy nation," and "a people for God's own possession" (2:9).

Submission—the voluntary yielding of oneself to another for a higher purpose than one's self–interest—is a major theme of *1 Peter*. While Christians remain in ultimate submission to Christ, this does not nullify or render unnecessary their submission to various people, relationships, or authorities. As citizens, we are to submit to governing authorities (2:13); as slaves, to masters (2:18); as wives, to our husbands (3:1); as

---

6   Adapted from C. H. Dodd, as quoted in Barclay, *Letters*, 167–168.

husbands, to our wives' femininity (3:7); as believers, to one another (3:8–9, etc.); as teachers, to those who need to be taught (3:15); as members of a given congregation, to our elders (5:1–4); as elders, to our "flock" *and* to Christ, the "Chief Shepherd" (5:4); and as "younger men," to older men (5:5). The purpose of all such submission is to maintain a proper attitude and an excellent behavior (2:12, 3:1–2, 3:16, etc.) amid a crooked world filled with "unreasonable" or crooked people (2:18).

The occasion of suffering—not merely the prospect of it, but the full expectation and reality of it—permeates Peter's writing.[7] The fact that Christians are distinctly different *from* the world invites the general hostility *of* the world. We will, then, be faced with "various trials" of faith (1:6)—not merely trials of different kinds, but also those of differing degrees of severity—just as Jesus warned would happen (John 15:18–20).[8] Instead of being spared from such open hostility, Christians are to prepare for and willingly accept it when it comes. Very similar to Paul's and James' admonitions (see Rom. 8:16–17 and James 1:2–4, respectively), Peter encourages a big–picture perspective toward suffering that looks well beyond the actual suffering itself (4:12–14):

---

7   Peter's authorship of *1 Peter* has been questioned by some simply because he is not *specific* as to the suffering to which he alludes. There are those who would expect Peter to say something about the brief but potent persecution that Emperor Nero unleashed upon Christians in Rome and elsewhere, since this happened in his lifetime; since he did not, therefore the author must not be Peter but someone writing later (even considerably later) under his name. But it is wearying to hear Bible critics citing all the things that they expected the Bible authors to say, and then to judge them (or dismiss them altogether) based simply upon such expectations. "If the necessary facts to establish a point in history are absent, scholars do well to avoid making dogmatic statements" (Simon J. Kistemaker, *New Testament Commentary: Exposition of the Epistles of Peter and the Epistle of Jude* [Grand Rapids: Baker Book House, 1987], 7). This is as true for Bible students as it is for Bible scholars—and Christians in general.

8   Peter refers to various forms of persecutions four times: 1 Peter 1:6–7, 3:13–17, 4:12–19, and 5:9. Not all these necessarily refer to the same historical occasion(s). Peter looks back on what has happened, looks forward to what lies ahead, and takes into account what is happening presently (at the time of his writing). It is also not clear as to whether these persecutions are initiated by Jews, or the Roman government, or both. In any case, Christians are called to endure these ordeals, and will be rewarded for doing so.

Beloved, do not be surprised at the fiery ordeal among you, which comes upon you for your testing, as though some strange thing were happening to you; but to the degree that you share the sufferings of Christ, keep on rejoicing, so that also at the revelation of His glory you may rejoice with exultation. If you are reviled for the name of Christ, you are blessed, because the Spirit of glory and of God rests on you.

Not only should the believer expect to suffer for the name of Christ, Peter says that he has been "called for this purpose, since Christ also suffered for you, leaving you an example for you to follow in His steps" (2:21). As Christ entrusted Himself to God's vindication of His integrity (2:23), faithful Christians who suffer injustices for the name of Christ should know that they will be compensated by a righteous God (4:19). This requires strong faith in this future vindication, for it likely will not happen in this life.

To clarify: Peter is *not* talking about *all* suffering, or what is broadly referred to as "human suffering." Thus, he is *not* saying, "Whoever suffers in this life for any reason, or whoever is the victim of any injustice, will be rewarded with eternal life in the world to come," as is popularly believed. Rather, the context is very specific: he speaks of the suffering of *Christians* while honoring God with their obedient faith (3:13–14 and 4:14; cf. Mat. 5:10–12, in principle). In fact, Peter pointedly dismisses any suffering that is the result of one's own refusal to be submissive (2:20) or his ungodly behavior (4:15). Such suffering is well deserved; there is nothing honorable in it. In contrast, "if anyone suffers as a Christian, he is not to be ashamed, but is to glorify God in this name" (4:16).

Such language impresses upon the believer the strong realization that this world is not his home, and therefore whatever happens *to* him is not as important as where he is going. The idea of Christians being "aliens" or "strangers" to the world reverberates throughout Peter's epistle. While the term is used only a few times (1:1 and 2:11), the *idea* is used repeatedly. Peter's message is, essentially, "You (Christians) do not belong to this world, yet you still reside here. And while you *are* here, you are morally obligated to conduct yourselves in such a way that does not compromise your faith or bring reproach upon your Savior."

Moral purity is a necessary virtue for one's submission to God (1:13–16, 2:1–2, 2:11–12, etc.). The Christian's inheritance has nothing to do with the material world or the human realm but lies with God in His world (1:4; cf. Eph. 2:19 and Heb. 11:13). Yet, until that inheritance is fully realized, Peter instructs Christians to "conduct yourselves in fear during the time of your stay on earth" (1:17). The epistles of *1 Peter* and *James* both converge on the need to do what is right, even to one's own harm (or, suffering), as summed up in 1 Peter 3:13–17 and James 1:2–12, respectively.

This perspective requires more than just waiting until that inheritance is given; it demands that believers "live the rest of the time in the flesh no longer for the lusts of men, but for the will of God" (4:2). With allegiance comes spiritual responsibility; such responsibility brings suffering and submission; endurance of these things brings transformation; and through such transformation we are made ready to live forever with God. Thus, "After you have suffered for a little while, the God of all grace, who called you to His eternal glory in Christ, will Himself perfect, confirm, strengthen and establish you" (5:10). Peter speaks repeatedly about Christ's Second Coming, always keeping it in the forefront of his thoughts; "It [Christ's return] is the motive for steadfastness in the faith, for the loyal living of the Christian life, and for gallant endurance amidst the sufferings, which have come, and which will come upon them [believers]."[9]

Author and Date: Simon Peter, also known as Cephas (John 1:42), is almost unanimously understood to be the author of *1 Peter*. Numerous early church "fathers" quoted from this epistle and attributed those quotes to Peter: Polycarp, Papias, Irenaeus, Clement of Alexandria, Origen, and Tertullian, as well as the early church historian Eusebius.[10]

---

9   Barclay, *Letters*, 165; bracketed words are mine.

10   JFB, *Commentary* (electronic), "Introduction." "Eusebius [ca. AD 260–339] states

Internal evidence also points to Peter, especially in referring to himself as an apostle (1:1), a witness of Christ's sufferings (5:1), and the style of writing that is consistent with Peter's sermons and statements in *Acts*. The external evidence "is seen in the fact that it [this letter] was universally recognized as written by him. No book has earlier or stronger evidence than 1 Peter."[11] Michaels agrees: "Aside from the four Gospels and the letters of Paul, the external attestation for 1 Peter is as strong, or stronger, than that for any NT book. There is no evidence anywhere of controversy over its authorship or authority."[12]

Peter himself was a native of Bethsaida, a small town on the Sea of Galilee, in a region in which Jesus personally ministered. His father was John (a.k.a. Jonah) (Mat. 16:17, John 1:42), and his brother was Andrew (Mat. 10:2, John 1:40). Both Peter and Andrew were fishermen by trade and worked in conjunction with the brothers James and John, who were also fishermen (Mat. 4:18–21). Upon meeting Peter for the first time, Jesus changed his name from Simon to "Peter" (in Aramaic, "Cephas," meaning "a small stone").[13] All the NT writers use "Peter" to identify

---

it as the opinion of those before him that this was among the universally acknowledged Epistles" (*ibid.*; bracketed words are mine). "We find abundant evidence of its [1 Peter's] influence on the thought and expression of early Christians, much of its wide reception and general recognition as Peter's, and none whatever that it was ever attributed to anyone else" (Alan M. Stibbs, *Tyndale New Testament Commentary: The First General Epistle of Peter* [Grand Rapids: Wm. B. Eerdmans Publishing Co., 1983], 18). Specific references of early church writers and "fathers" are listed in detail in J. Ramsey Michaels, *Word Biblical Commentary, vol. 49: 1 Peter* (Waco, TX: Word Books, 1988), xxi–xxxiii.

11   Cogdill, *Book by Book*, 153; bracketed words are mine.

12   Michaels, *Word Biblical Commentary*, xxxiv.

13   While "Cephas" means simply "rock," "Peter" [*petros*] means "a small stone." In Mat. 16:18, Jesus uses two different words that are related but not interchangeable. *Petros* (a small stone) is Peter's name; *petra* ("upon this <u>rock</u>") refers not to a small stone but to a large rock mass. Peter was the confessor of Jesus' true role ("the Christ") and nature ("the Son of the living God"); it was not Peter upon whom Jesus built His church, but the truth of this confession. While many will say that "Cephas" has no distinction as to size or mass, still it is Matthew—an apostle and divinely inspired author—who wrote his gospel in Greek and made the differentiation between the two. This point alone ought to end all controversy on the matter, but sadly many (including the entire Catholic religion) have turned to this passage to support Peter as

him, except for Paul (1 Cor. 1:12, Gal. 2:9, etc.). Jesus named Peter as one of His twelve apostles, and he often served—often, it appears, on his own initiative—as a spokesman for the other eleven. He was married (1 Cor. 9:5), but we do not know his wife's name; according to tradition, she, like her husband, also faced martyrdom.[14]

When we are first introduced to Peter, he appears to be an assertive, impetuous, and zealous man. Yet, he was also very conscious of his own sins and failings (Luke 5:1–11) and remained, except for the time of Jesus' trials, devoted to his Lord and Master (John 6:66–69). He was vocal and straightforward but did not always show discretion in what he said. He personally rebuked Jesus—the only person in Scripture to do so!—for what He said regarding what would happen to Him in Jerusalem, and Jesus soundly rebuked him in return (Mat. 16:21–23). (Jesus had many names for the Pharisees, but he never called them "Satan"; yet this is what he called Peter!) God Himself rebuked Peter for suggesting that three equal "tabernacles" be built for Jesus, Moses, and Elijah (Mat. 17:1–5). Later, Peter proudly declared that he would stand by Jesus till the end and even die with Him (Luke 22:33); yet, when given opportunity to do so only hours later, three times he denied even knowing Jesus (Luke 22:54–62). Unfortunately, Peter's boldness and courage were easily overcome by fear (Mat. 14:30) and the opinions of others (Gal. 2:11–14).

Yet, Peter continued to grow in his faith and mature in his resolve, and he served as a spokesman for the apostles and the early church from Acts 1 forward. After His resurrection and before He was received into heaven, Jesus restored Peter's place, so to speak, as the leader of the twelve (John 21:15–17). As a first order of business, Peter headed the appointment of Matthias to replace Judas Iscariot, who had committed suicide (Acts 1:15–26). He also preached the first and second recorded

---

being the man upon which Christ founded His entire church—a man who would later vehemently deny Him three times (!). Scripture is emphatically clear that Jesus is the "chief cornerstone" upon which His church is built, not Peter (1 Peter 2:4–7).

14 JFB, *Commentary* (electronic), "Introduction"; apparently this is sourced from Clement of Alexandria.

gospel sermons to the Jews in Jerusalem (Acts 2, 3). Peter and John were the first Christians to be arrested in Jerusalem for preaching Christ (Acts 4); later, all the apostles were arrested, but Peter remained their chief spokesman (Acts 5:17–32).[15]

After the great dispersion of Christians from Jerusalem following Stephen's martyrdom (Acts 8:1–4), Peter assumed a more independent ministry, traveling outside of the city and eventually outside of Judea (Acts 9:31–43). Even so, under Peter's watch and through his preaching, the Gentiles were accepted into the church (Acts 10), fulfilling his role as the one with "the keys of the kingdom" (Mat. 16:19). Herod Agrippa I, to please the Jews, had the apostle James arrested and then executed. He then arrested Peter with full intention to execute him as well, but God intervened and rescued him from prison (Acts 12:1–19)—the second time He had done so (see Acts 5:17–20).

Peter was one of the primary speakers in resolving the debate with certain Pharisees in the so–called council in Jerusalem (Acts 15:7–11). Yet, this is the last time we hear of him in *Acts*, as the narrative focuses instead upon Paul from that point forward. We do hear of him incidentally thereafter (1 Cor. 1:12, 9:5, 15:5, and Gal. 2:11–14), but it is not until the writing of *1 Peter* do we hear from him directly.[16] Some

---

15   "The Greek of the Epistle [of 1 Peter] if formally good, rhythmic, polished and elegant… Now the Peter of the Gospels is a Galilean fisherman, who normally speaks Aramaic with an unmistakable north–country accent. He is explicitly described in Acts 4:13 as 'unlearned and ignorant.' Even allowing for some improvement in Greek which missionary work in Gentile areas—commenced, incidentally, rather late in life—would bring, could he be responsible for such delicate balance of phrase and felicitous choice of words?" (Stibbs, *TNTC*, 23). Stibbs offers this rhetorically since he does not believe the critique to hold weight. The Jews' reference to Peter (and John) being unlearned likely refers to their lack of formal rabbinic training, not illiteracy. A plausible theory, too, is that Silvanus (Silas) is the actual secretary of this letter (see comments on 5:12), in which case Peter dictated it to him and he framed Peter's words in the polished style that we now read (*ibid.*, 26–27). We also must not dismiss whatever provision God made for Peter to be able to write a letter such as this. If God can make men speak in tongues they had never learned (Acts 2:1–12), certainly He can make men write in ways that exceeded their natural ability.

16   Common topics in Peter's speeches in Acts (chapters 2 – 5) resurface in *1 Peter*, namely: Christ's fulfillment of the OT Scriptures (1:10–12); the resurrection

early church traditions claim that Peter went to Rome and established a church there, but this cannot be substantiated, and often the dates and details put forward are in serious conflict with historical facts. Jesus prophesied that Peter would face martyrdom (John 21:18–19), and tradition says that he did so, in Rome (ca. AD 68), because of Emperor Nero's brief but fiery persecution against the church.[17]

First Peter is thought to have been written late in Peter's life, likely during some intense persecution in the Anatolian Peninsula (based on 1:6–9 and 4:12), but it is not clear whether this persecution is from the Jews or the Roman government.[18] The fact that he refers to himself as "a fellow elder" among the other church elders (5:1) indicates a man who is in the later season of his life. Most conservative scholarship places the date around AD 63–64, which seems to be a very reasonable conclusion.

---

and exaltation of Christ (1:3, 21); the call to repentance (or, holy living) (1:13–16); the importance of baptism (3:21–22); and the certainty of Christ's judgment of humankind (4:4–5).

17 John Foxe, *Foxe's Book of Martyrs* (Roanoke, VA: Scripture Truth, no date), 12–13.

18 Barclay has extensive—and excellent—information on the Neronian persecution that began in Rome in AD 64 (*Letters*, 173–189). This persecution was in connection to the burning of Rome, for which Nero was responsible, though he blamed Christians. This long and involved historical detail goes beyond my commentary but is well worth reading for a better understanding of the real and dangerous trials the early church faced. On the other hand, there is nothing specific in *1 & 2 Peter* that alludes directly to this specific persecution, or to the persecution of the church due to emperor worship (which did not surface until very late in the first century). Thus, it seems more reasonable to believe that Peter's audience in the Anatolian Peninsula faced a persecution that was either an extension of the Jewish persecution detailed in Acts, or something about which we know nothing else.

General Outline

- Salutation (1:1–2)
- A Living Hope (1:3–12)
- A Holy People (1:13 – 2:3)
- A People for God's Own Possession (2:4–12)
- A General Call to Submission (2:13–25)
- Submission in Marriage (3:1–7)
- Living with a Good Conscience (3:8–22)
- Practical Application of Righteous Living (4:1–11)
- The Expectation of Suffering (4:12–19)
- Final Exhortations (5:1–10)
- Closing Remarks (5:11–14)

Salutation
(1 Peter 1:1–2)

"Peter, an apostle of Jesus Christ…" (1:1a)—the author immediately states his identity and authority. We have no good reason to believe that this is anyone other than Simon Peter (a.k.a. Cephas) who is well-known to us in the gospels and Acts (see "Introduction"). To speak as an apostle of Christ is, in essence, to have Him speaking. This does not mean that the apostles' authority is on par with Christ's, but that He has given them authority to speak in His name.

Peter's original readers are "aliens [or strangers; pilgrims; exiles; or sojourners]" who are scattered abroad.[19] This alludes historically to what is known as the Jewish Diaspora—the dispersion of Israelites throughout the Roman Empire for various reasons over the several prior centuries. The implication, however, refers to *spiritual* "Israelites" who have become citizens of the kingdom of God through their conversion to Christ.[20] Peter has no reason to write to unconverted Jews; the content of the letter also prevents him from writing exclusively to Jewish Christians. Thus, the natural and necessarily implied reference here is to Christians—whether Jewish or Gentile—who reside throughout the geographical regions he is about to name.[21] "Christians are thus

---

19   In the Greek text, the word "elect" or "chosen" appears in front of "strangers"; thus, "to the elect strangers" (Albert Barnes, *Barnes' Notes on the New Testament*, electronic edition [database © 2014 by WORDsearch], on 1:1). But several translations, including the NASB (which is the primary citation for our present study), put "who are chosen" after the naming of the provinces to clarify *how* and *why* these "strangers" were chosen. This new placement in no way changes the original meaning, however, and is thus perfectly acceptable.

20   "Those exiled Jews were called the *Diaspora*, the dispersion. But now the real Diaspora is not the Jewish nation; the real Diaspora is the Christian Church scattered abroad throughout the provinces of the Roman Empire and the nations of the world. Once the people who had been different from other peoples was the Jews; now the people who are different are the Christians. They are the people whose King is God, and whose home is eternity, and who are strangers, sojourners, and exiles in the world" (Barclay, *Letters*, 196–197).

21   This is the same conclusion that one draws concerning the "bond–servants of

challenged by Peter's opening address to think of themselves as citizens of heaven, and only 'strangers and pilgrims' here."[22]

Some commentators see a travel itinerary implied in the order in which the five Roman provinces—Pontus, Galatia, Cappadocia, Asia (Minor), and Bithynia—are listed. To some, this implies that Peter was writing from somewhere in the east (from actual Babylon?—see comments on 5:13) and wrote these in the order that he would see them on a map. Others suggest that Silvanus (Silas), the bearer of this letter (5:12), would travel this route on his way from the east as he crossed the Anatolian Peninsula and boarded a ship for Rome somewhere on the western shore of Asia Minor.[23]

On the other hand, such conjectures are a lot to conclude from simply a list of provinces. It is also possible that Peter is simply reciting them from how he remembers them, tracing the provinces as one might trace in his mind a group of states or countries in our present time. Most of these provinces are also mentioned in Acts 2:9–11 and suggest that the gospel message that was preached by Peter on Pentecost was then carried back to those peoples' homelands and took root, possibly with churches being formed as a result. We also know that Paul may have established some of these churches in Galatia and Asia Minor, especially if one of these churches is in Ephesus (the capital of Asia Minor). What this means is: Paul and Peter are both ministering in their own way to the same territories.

These Christians are "aliens" to the unconverted world, but they are no strangers to God. In fact, they are "chosen" by Him through their obedient response to His gospel (1:1b–2). "Chosen" (or "elect") here must be understood in the context of the entire New Testament (NT) as a distinct reference to Christian believers in general. Whenever "chosen" is used to describe Christians, it is always with respect to a group, never

---

God"—i.e., Christians, with no actual reference to ethnicity—who are nonetheless symbolically associated with Israelite tribes in Rev. 7:2–8.

22   Stibbs, *TNTC*, 72.

23   JFB, *Commentary* (electronic), on 1:1.

to an individual.[24] Thus, all these "strangers" are chosen *as a group*—that is, they are strangers with respect to where they live (in Pontus, etc.), but not as a unique people. *All* believers are "strangers and exiles on the earth" (Heb. 11:13), and as such, they *all* belong to the great multitude of believers worldwide. The "chosen" are not pre-selected by God to be saved regardless of their will, as Calvinism teaches, but are "chosen" because of who they have become (Christians), who they are identified with (Christ), and whose fellowship they now enjoy (God's). The following verses are consistent with this idea (emphases are all mine):

❑ "Blessed be the God and Father of our Lord Jesus Christ, who has blessed us with every spiritual blessing in the heavenly places in Christ, just as He chose us in Him before the foundation of the world, that we would be holy and blameless before Him." (Eph. 1:3–4)
❑ "So, as those who have been chosen of God, holy and beloved, put on a heart of compassion, kindness, humility, gentleness and patience…" (Col. 3:12)
❑ "But we should always give thanks to God for you, brethren beloved by the Lord, because God has chosen you from the beginning for salvation through sanctification by the Spirit and faith in the truth. It was for this He called you through our gospel, that you may gain the glory of our Lord Jesus Christ." (2 Thess. 2:13–14)
❑ "For this reason I endure all things for the sake of those who are chosen, so that they also may obtain the salvation which is in Christ Jesus and with it eternal glory." (2 Tim. 2:10)
❑ "Paul, a bond-servant of God and an apostle of Jesus Christ, for the faith of those chosen of God and the knowledge of the truth which is according to godliness…." (Titus 1:1)
❑ "But you are a chosen race, a royal priesthood, a holy nation, a people for God's own possession, so that you may proclaim the excellencies of Him who has called you out of darkness into His

---

24 John's reference to "the chosen [or, elect] lady" in 2 John 1:1 does not violate this point, since this "lady" most likely refers to a church, not a specific person. For a thorough explanation on this, I recommend my *1–2–3 John and Jude Commentary* (2024); go to www.spiritbuilding.com/chad.

marvelous light…" (1 Peter 2:9)

❑ "These will wage war against the Lamb, and the Lamb will overcome them, because He is Lord of lords and King of kings, and those who are with Him are the called and chosen and faithful." (Rev. 19:14)

In every citation above, "chosen" refers to a group of people—either a geographical collection of Christians (as in *2 Thessalonians*) or all Christians everywhere (as in *2 Timothy*). Nowhere in the NT is it taught that God chooses people to be saved *apart from their own choice to obey Him*, or that He condemns people to be lost *regardless of their desire to be saved*. Both ideas are major points of Calvinism, but they are unbiblical and contradict the free will of every person either to accept God's invitation of salvation or reject it.

There is no question, however, that God is the One who does the "choosing." The point of controversy is not whether Christians *are* chosen by God, for they most certainly are, but whether they have any moral responsibility or personal decision on their part to become part *of* the chosen of God. "According to the foreknowledge of God the Father" does not mean, "God knows all of whom will be chosen" (although He can know this as well), but that the *fact that the choice is offered* is predicated upon God's divine grace. Foreknowledge is not the same as forcing the issue; to foreknow something does not mean you make it happen, but that you know ahead of time that it *will* happen, given the right conditions and opportunities (Acts 2:23). God knows (or foreknows) that He will call people to Himself through His gospel; He also foreknows that those who rightly respond to His call will become the "chosen" of God. But He does not force anyone to be saved (or chosen) any more than He denies anyone who calls upon His name for salvation (Acts 2:21, Rom. 10:11–13, etc.).

To further underscore this idea, Peter identifies three necessary conditions to those who are "chosen"—though not in sequential order (1:2):

- "by the sanctifying work of the Spirit"—i.e., the act of consecrating and setting apart those who have been called by God and responded in faith. "Sanctify" means "to make holy"; those who are sanctified are known thereafter as "saints." The sanctification process is what the Holy Spirit performs upon those who are "in Christ" (1 Cor. 1:2, 2 Thess. 2:13), having been "washed" through the act of water baptism as an act of faith (1 Cor. 6:11, Titus 3:5, Heb. 10:22, etc.).
- "to obey Jesus Christ"—because no one can become part of the "chosen" who will not obey Christ (John 15:12–14, 1 John 2:3–4, etc.). Whatever Christ requires of us is what we are to obey; all forms of obedience to Him are considered acts of faith.
- "and be sprinkled with His blood"—the allusion here is to the Law of Moses, in which the high priest would sprinkle blood upon the mercy seat of the ark of the covenant during the Day of Atonement observance (Lev. 16:11–16).[25] In that occurrence, animal blood was sprinkled for the purpose of making atonement—first, for the high priest; second, for the nation of Israel. But the NT writers have applied this same language to the act of atonement through the blood of Christ (cf. Heb. 10:22 and 12:24). The "sprinkling" is now figurative, but the application of the blood to the guilty soul is quite real.[26]

In a brief but powerful manner, Peter has laid out the theological foundation for those who belong to Christ (the "chosen" or "elect"). Such people are called by the Father, sanctified by the Spirit, and cleansed by the Son's blood. The order is out of sequence—atonement *always* and *necessarily* precedes consecration—but it is not Peter's point to make a sequential statement, only a truthful and descriptive one. "May grace and peace be yours…"—those who are chosen by God and stand in His favor are recipients of divine grace; it cannot be otherwise.

25　There may also be an allusion here to the blood of the covenant which was sprinkled upon the book of the covenant itself, the altar upon which the blood sacrifice was made, and the people who swore allegiance to the covenant (Exod. 24:1–8; see Heb. 9:18–22).

26　This does not mean that the application is happening in real time; it means that this *must be done* for that soul to be cleansed of its sins. "…[A]ll things are cleansed with blood, and without shedding of blood there is no forgiveness" (Heb. 9:22).

And, those who are saved by grace are also at peace with God, since they are in His fellowship (Rom. 5:1–2). "Peter's brief greeting, 'Grace and peace be yours in abundance,' gives in miniature the whole message of his letter."[27]

A Living Hope
(1 Peter 1:3–12)

Born Again Believers (1:3–5): Peter formally and fittingly begins his epistle with what Lenski calls a "great doxology,"[28] or hymn of praise: "Blessed be the God and Father…" (1:3a). "Blessed" here means to speak good words toward (someone); it is recognition of someone who is (or is to be) well-spoken of.[29] Peter also says in clear and unmistakable language that God *is* Jesus' Father, and therefore Jesus *is* the Son of God. In fact, whoever denies that Jesus is the Son of God is a liar and an "antichrist" (see 1 John 2:22–23). In divine mercy—"mercy" being that which spares us from what we deserve—God provided a way for sinners to regain their fellowship with Him. This refers to a spiritual rebirth (being "born again") in which the soul dies to its allegiance to sin and is reborn into a new allegiance to Christ. (This was alluded to in John 3:3–5 and explained in Rom. 6:3–7.)

Those who live according "to the course of this [sinful] world" are "dead" to God's fellowship (Eph. 2:1–2). By dying to the world—and thus, to the condemnation that one's law-breaking has brought upon him (Rom. 7:4)—a person is reborn into a new fellowship with God that is based upon different terms and conditions than the fellowship he once had

---

27 Edmund Clowney, *The Message of 1 Peter* (Downers Grove, IL: InterVarsity Press, 1988), 27.

28 R. C. H. Lenski, *Commentary on the New Testament: The Interpretation of the Epistles of St. Peter, St. John, and Jude* (Peabody, MA: Hendrickson Publishers, 1998), 28.

29 Marvin R. Vincent, *Vincent's Word Studies in the New Testament*, electronic edition (database © 2014 by WORDsearch), on 1:3. Paul uses the same phrase in 2 Cor. 1:3 and Eph. 1:3.

prior to his ever having sinned against Him. Thus, one must die to the *world*, must die with *Christ* (Rom. 6:4, 2 Tim. 2:11), and then must be resurrected to a *new life* with God *in* Christ (Eph. 2:4–7).

This new relationship is determined by a covenant agreement between God and the one who calls upon His name for salvation. God offers the terms of that salvation in His gospel; the sinner either accepts or rejects those terms. Being "born again" is not a mere spiritual concept, religious revival, or emotional experience; it is the real, historical, and life–changing point in time when a person renounces self–will and his love for the world, and openly declares his loving allegiance to Christ. The *defining act* of this event is his baptism into Christ. One who refuses to be baptized into Christ also defies the method by which a person becomes a Christ–follower (i.e., a Christian). The popular idea of "just ask Jesus into your heart to be your personal Savior" is unbiblical and hopeless. One cannot be "born of God" (John 1:12–13) without doing what *God* says is necessary for that rebirth.

Being "born again" provides something the sinner did not have before: *hope*. (Those who die outside of Christ—i.e., outside of a covenant relationship with God *through* Christ—have "no hope" or are "without hope"; see Eph. 2:12, 4:17–19, and 1 Thess. 4:13.) Peter goes one step further and calls this a "*living* hope" (emphasis added). This is because it is based upon the perpetual, ever–living intercession of Jesus Christ (Heb. 7:23–28); it inspires life, love, and obedience in the believer (Rom. 5:1–5); and it anticipates eternal life with God (Rom. 8:24–25).

While the believer's hope looks forward to what lies ahead, it is predicated on the reality of what has been done to secure it—namely, "the resurrection of Jesus Christ from the dead" (1:3b). If Christ had not been raised from the dead, then this would indicate that God did not have the power to raise Him, He did not have the *desire* to raise Him, and/or Christ really was not who He said He was—the Son of God. The entirety of the Christian faith rests upon Christ's resurrection. If He has not been raised, then our conscience remains corrupted (1 Peter 3:21–22); we are still in our sins (1 Cor. 15:17); our faith and our preaching is "in vain" (1 Cor. 15:14); we cannot walk in "newness of life" (Rom. 6:4); we will not be raised (1 Cor. 6:14); etc. Likewise, we cannot have a "living hope" apart from Christ's own irrepressible life: because He lives, therefore we can live, and, if we remain faithful to our covenant with God, *will* live with Him forever.

Peter then tells the "born again" believer what he can look forward to (1:4): "an inheritance." The reasons why Christians are called "sons of God"—emphasis being on the word *sons* here—is because of our being qualified for an inheritance (Gal. 3:26–27, Col. 1:12). The NT language concerning our spiritual inheritance imitates that of the ancient world in which firstborn sons received a double inheritance and all other sons received whatever remained. (Daughters only received an inheritance if there were no sons; see Num. 27:1–11.) Christ has received the Father's *full* inheritance, since He is the "only begotten Son" of God (John 1:14, 3:16, Heb. 1:2, etc.), and He promises to share His inheritance with all who are adopted sons of God. If we are "born again," then we are "sons" of God; otherwise, we have no inheritance to look forward to; and if we have no inheritance, then we have nothing to hope for in the life to come.

The Christian's inheritance is a magnificent one (1:4). It is "imperishable"—it cannot die or be corrupted; "So many inheritances vanish away before they are obtained."[30] It is "undefiled"—it has no flaw, defect, or blemish that would render it unfit to receive. It "will not fade away"—it will not be diminished by time, circumstances, the elements, or natural deterioration. This is because there is nothing natural about this inheritance; it is not of this world, just as Jesus' kingdom is not of this world (John 18:36). Accordingly, it is "reserved in heaven"—far from the reach of anyone or anything that might corrupt it (Mat. 6:20).

---

30   A. T. Robertson, *Word Pictures in the New Testament*, electronic edition (© 1960 by The Sunday School Board of the Southern Baptist Convention; database © 2007 by WORDsearch Corp.), on 1:4. Barclay says that "imperishable" here can have another meaning, namely, unravaged by any invading army. "Many and many a time the land of Palestine had been ravaged by the armies of the aliens; it had been fought over and blasted and destroyed; but the Christian possesses a peace, a joy, a safety, a serenity which no invading army can ravage and destroy" (*Letters*, 204–5).

And this inheritance is "for you"—think of it: *for you!* This is not some promise made to someone else, or something that you strongly desire but are helpless to receive. This is God's promise to *all* who live faithful to Him and put their full confidence in His ability to perform (Rom. 4:21).

Faithful Christians do not just believe in God; we are also protected by His divine power (1:5). We have needs, God provides fulfillment; we have enemies, God provides security; we have fears and doubts, God provides confidence and peace; we have human limitations, God provides divine strength to overcome them (2 Cor. 12:9–10). This providence is contingent, however, upon our continued faith in Him ("through faith"). Since we "are all sons of God through faith in Christ Jesus" (Gal. 3:26), therefore we are also promised an inheritance that God will guard until it is finally and fully received. Peter says, in effect, "You do not have to worry about your spiritual inheritance. God has your future all under control, if you but trust His plans for you and believe in what He has promised you."

Our salvation has not yet been revealed, but there is a day coming—God guarantees it—when it will be revealed (or, made fully visible) to us. For now, it is ours in promise and by faith; in due time, it will be ours in full and in fact. The only thing Peter adds to this revealing is that it will occur "in the last time"—undoubtedly, the day in which we stand before Christ and give an account of our life here on earth (2 Cor. 5:10, Rev. 20:11–15).

The Refining of Our Faith (1:6–9): Such a grand inheritance is cause for rejoicing among those to whom it has been promised (1:6).[31] Yet, Peter recognizes that just because Christians have an excellent future in the life to come does not make all the problems of this life evaporate. In many cases, being a faithful Christian *increases* life's troubles,

---

31   With reference to 1:3–9, Lenski says: "First, certainty; next, joy. First, living hope, an inheritance safely kept for us in heaven, and we ourselves kept for this inheritance; next, while we wait, joy despite trials, these trials only refining us like gold. The grand doxology simply moves forward…" (*Interpretation*, 37).

responsibilities, and strain. Specifically, Peter refers to the "various trials" of the believer's faith in God, up to and including religious persecution (as does James in a parallel thought—James 1:2–4). He does, however, contrast the limited scope of those troubles in comparison to the timeless and numerous blessings of one's life with God in heaven (cf. 2 Cor. 4:16–18). These first things are "for a little while"; the latter things are forever. These first things will happen only "if necessary"; the latter things will happen *for certain*. It is God who controls both sides of the picture: He protects the believer on earth, but allows him (or her) to undergo what is necessary for his faith to grow larger and stronger; He also protects his future inheritance, so that when this relatively short life is over, the believer will be ushered into heavenly glory (Rom. 8:18, Col. 3:1–4, and 1 Peter 5:10).

Peter is not patronizing his readers ("What are you so worked up about? They're just a few 'trials,' nothing more!"). Instead, he is being realistic. The trials are real—and distressing. The suffering is real—and upsetting. The temptation to sin (including the sin of unbelief; see Heb. 3:12 – 4:2) is real—and can be spiritually exhausting. The struggle to maintain a healthy faith here on earth is often met with periods of doubt, uncertainty, anxiousness, and other forms of fear. Many Christians have privately wondered, "If God cares so much about me, why is He letting me be faced with such difficult trials?" Peter's manifold response to all of this (1:7–9):

- ❑ The "proof [or, genuineness; authenticity] of your faith" (1:7) is necessary to know where one's loyalty lies. He who wishes to keep his own life compromises his loyalty to Christ; he who has left this world behind and follows Christ with all his heart will endure sufferings for His name's sake (Mat. 5:10–12, 16:24–25). Faith that is never tested is not really "faith" at all but empty words. It is not until one is forced to cling to his faith tenaciously—especially while incurring personal pain or loss—that his faith begins to take shape and solidify.
- ❑ Human faith in God is "more precious than gold" (1:7)—not only to God, but also to the one who possesses it. Gold is limited

to this world; its value is determined by people, availability, and economics. Obedient faith, however, looks beyond this world; its value is determined by God, regardless of earthly factors. Since ancient times, gold has been extracted from iron ore and other inferior materials through smelting. This process involves heating up the rock so that the gold liquifies and pours out of it, providing the smelter with pure gold. The same is true with Christians: various trials of faith, being faced with temptations, wrestling with fears and doubts, and actual persecution, heat up our lives, so to speak. As a result, our faith—if it is real and enduring—pours out of us and is given to God as a kind of offering (in essence, a "living and holy sacrifice"—Rom. 12:1) which, in God's eyes, is *priceless* as much as it is *honorable* to Him. Gold is perishable, since it can and will be destroyed; but faith is imperishable, in that it can endure trials, human assaults, spiritual warfare, and the test of time.

❑ Thus, while we are beset with "fire," the excellent outcome serves to praise God (1:7). The message to Him is, "You, my God, are *worthy* of my going through the crucible to prove my loyalty and faith to You." The praise we give to God in this form will be returned to us in due time: we will be rewarded in the form of praise (words), glory (recognition), and honor (action) when finally presented before the Father and His Son in the Judgment. "The revelation of Jesus Christ" literally refers to the event in which Jesus is visibly revealed to us and the rest of the world (see Acts 1:9–11, 1 Thess. 2:19, 2 Thess. 1:6–8, 2:1, and Rev. 1:7).[32]

❑ Christians do not need to see Jesus *now*, however, to believe in Him (1:8). In fact, "even though we [i.e., eyewitnesses of Jesus during His ministry—MY WORDS] have known Christ according to the flesh, yet now we know Him in this way no longer" (2 Cor. 5:16). Yet, Jesus said to Thomas, "Because you have seen Me, have you believed? Blessed are they who did not see, and yet believed" (John 20:29). Many say that "seeing is believing"; in the present case, "believing is

---

32 "The use of [Greek] *apokalupsis*, 'appearing' (RSV, 'revelation'), suggests not the 'coming' of someone hitherto [or, up to this point] absent, but the visible unveiling or disclosure of someone who has been all the time spiritually and invisibly present" (Stibbs, *TNTC*, 78–9; bracketed words are mine).

seeing." When we believe in Jesus because of what others have seen, preached, recorded, and even died for, He becomes alive to us—we "see" Him. This is what God expects of us, given that "we walk by faith, not by sight" (2 Cor. 5:7).

❏ Having "seen" Christ through the eyes of faith, we also *love* Him (1:8). Our love for Christ is not dependent upon Him providing a visible confirmation of His existence; the physical creation (Rom. 1:18–20) and the Bible record (John 20:31) are sufficient for this. "Millions, and hundreds of millions, have been led to love the Saviour, who have never seen him. They have seen—not with the bodily eye, but with the eye of faith—the inimitable beauty of his character, and have been brought to love him with an ardour of affection which they never had for any other one."[33] "By this the love of God was manifested in us, that God has sent His only begotten Son into the world so that we might live through Him" (1 John 4:9); likewise, our love for God is manifested in our willingness to endure various trials, hostilities, and injustices for His Son. Peter is not speaking theoretically here; he is writing to those whom he knows have endured the ordeals to which he refers. His exhortation addresses real people going through real trials for a very real faith.

The result of overcoming such trials of faith successfully is rejoicing "with joy inexpressible and full of glory [or simply, glorified]" (1:8).

Joy is a gift that we receive from God [because of His salvation—MY WORDS], for Scripture shows that God is the giver of joy (see Ps. 16:11, John 16:24, and Rom. 15:13). This gift, then, comes to the believer who puts his complete trust in God. Joy is a gift that must be shared with others. The shepherd who finds his sheep and the woman who finds her coin share their joy with neighbors, while the angels in heaven rejoice over one sinner who repents (Luke 15:4–10). In Scripture, joy is often related to God's almighty acts of saving man. As a result, man expresses his joy by loving God and by obeying his commands. And last, joy is [a] fruit of the Spirit (Gal. 5:22).[34]

---

33 Barnes, *Barnes' Notes* (electronic), on 1:8.

34 Kistemaker, *NTC*, 51.

One of the great paradoxes of Christianity is that joy comes through suffering: overcoming difficulties, triumphing in battle, and the satisfaction of doing what is right produce great joy in the one who sees past the trial itself and finds tremendous fulfillment in pleasing his God (as Jesus did—see Heb. 12:2–3).[35] The "outcome" of a faith that is willing to endure various trials and persecution is "the salvation of your souls" (1:9). This does not mean that all who suffer, or all who suffer for any kind of faith, are guaranteed salvation; the context and application are clearly defined. It is true that no one is saved by faith alone; it is also true that no one is saved who will not live by faith in God—a faith which needs to be validated by self–denial, sacrifice, and even suffering.

The Ancient Prophecies (1:10–12): In a kind of aside, Peter has something to say about this salvation (1:10–12). Clearly, the plan, means, and offering of salvation are not something for which the believers themselves are responsible. God has been working on this plan for a long time—indeed, "for all eternity" (2 Tim. 1:9, Eph. 3:11). God also unveiled this plan over a long period of time, gradually and methodically pulling back the curtain to reveal what ultimately would happen. But those to whom the gospel remained a mystery yet to be revealed—i.e., the ancient prophets—"made careful searches and inquiries" into the exact time and way God would reveal the world's Redeemer (1:10–11). Their prophecies were not their witness of Christ as much as His witness through them. They only received pieces and parts, not the whole picture; their view was dim and obscured, not bright and clear. This was especially true when God predicted that the Messiah would have to suffer before He would be exalted to glory (1:11). (This no doubt refers to such passages as Isa. 50:4–7 and 52:13 – 53:12; see Luke 24:25–27, 44–47.)

---

35   This needs to be further emphasized: there is, certainly, no joy *in* suffering, but joy comes *through* suffering. "Suffering produces sorrow, while joy is the result of vindication. In the present passage [1:8], suffering and sorrow belong to the present, while vindication and joy, although very near, belong to the future" (Michaels, *WBC*, 37). Christians are not to be masochists—people who *enjoy* pain and suffering. Rather, we are to be those who see past the present difficulty and live—or even die—in joyful anticipation of being with our Savior.

These men were prophets, to be sure, but they were seldom privileged to precisely know that of which they prophesied. Furthermore, they remained mere men, and thus had all the struggles, curiosities, and longings that all men have. Not only did they want to know *who* God was talking about, but *when* His plan would be fully revealed (see Dan. 12:8–9, for example). As Jesus told His disciples, "For truly I say to you that many prophets and righteous men desired to see what you see, and did not see it, and to hear what you hear, and did not hear it" (Mat. 13:17).

What God *did* reveal to His prophets was that they were not speaking of things pertaining to themselves (i.e., things that would have an immediate application in their lifetime, or anytime soon) (1:12). This is in specific reference to what are called the messianic prophecies—those pertaining to the time of the Messiah—not to every prophecy.

> Peter is not saying that the prophets had no ministry to their own time, or that they spoke in inspired riddles that made no sense to them or to their hearers. The very diligence of their search for better understanding shows how the prophecies challenged and intrigued them. What Peter is eager to point out is that his hearers are the heirs of the full message of the prophets.[36]

Thus, it is *Christians* who are the recipients of the full extent of all such prophecies: they are, in a sense, on the other side of the cross, and thus able to see in hindsight the full plan of God unfolded (Heb. 11:39–40). Furthermore, Christians have not mere prophets but hand–picked spokesmen (the apostles) to disclose the so–called "mystery of Christ" in the gospel message (Eph. 3:3–7). Many of the OT prophetic oracles concerning the restoration or regathering of Israel are in fact fulfilled in the church age, yet are purposely cloaked in mystery, obscurity, and (often) poetic language. "The whole New Testament gospel rests on the Spirit's Old Testament testimony that was made through the Old Testament prophets. Cancel that testimony, and you remove the basis of

---

36 Clowney, *Message*, 59.

the gospel of Christ."[37]

But now, "these things ... have been announced to you through those who preached the gospel to you" (1:12). The Holy Spirit is directly responsible for this preaching, not only in preparing those who would preach, but also the content of the preaching, and even the miracles that authenticate it (Heb. 2:3–4). He (the Spirit) was "sent from heaven" for this purpose—that is, He was given to the church by the Father at the Son's request, once He (Christ) had ascended to receive His throne (Acts 2:33).

Two things are especially striking in this passage (1:10–12). First, "the Spirit of Christ" and "the Holy Spirit" are used interchangeably, making it appear (at first glance) that Christ *is* the Holy Spirit. This cannot be true, since the Spirit is often mentioned in the NT as a third member of the Godhead with an individual name, personality, and role (as in 1:2; see 2 Cor. 13:14). But it *can* be true that the pre–incarnate Son of God and the Holy Spirit of God worked in seamless cooperation in providing the necessary (albeit shrouded) details to the prophets as to what would happen in their distant future. This seems the most natural, logical, and biblical explanation. It is also consistent with Rom. 8:9, where this same interchangeableness occurs. In that passage (read the full context: Rom. 8:6–11), it is unmistakable that "the Spirit of Christ" and "the Holy Spirit" are two distinctly different, yet fully cooperative, entities.

Second, the OT prophecies provoked the wonder and curiosity not only of human prophets, but also heavenly angels ("things into which angels long to look"—1:12).[38] We often assume that angels know everything God knows, that they are omniscient beings simply because they are in

---

37   Lenski, *Interpretation*, 49.

38   The word simply translated "look" comes from a Greek word (*parakupto*) which means, "to bend beside; to lean over (so as to peer within); to stoop down," to gain a better or clearer view (James Strong, *Strong's Talking Greek-Hebrew Dictionary*, electronic edition [database © WORDsearch Corp.], G3879). The same word is used to describe Peter's "stooping down" to get a better look into Jesus' empty tomb (Luke 24:12). Similarly, angels long(ed) to "stoop down" to gain a better understanding of the human world, and the dynamics of God's interaction with human beings.

heaven where God is. But there is nothing in Scripture to confirm this, and Scripture is the *only* authentic source of otherworldly information available to humankind. Nothing *factual* about the spiritual realm can be known except for what God has revealed to us.

Thus, while angels always seem to know far more than we do, this does not mean they know all things, or that God told them everything that He did not tell the ancient prophets. (The same can be said of *fallen* angels, and Satan in particular. We may assume that Satan knows everything, or fully knew of God's plan to offer His Son on the cross to defeat him, but there is nothing in Scripture that proves this. If anything, the implications take us in the opposite direction.[39])

While there are many things we do not know about the world of angels, there are also many things angels do not understand about what it means to be human. Furthermore, while angels are dispatched to carry out God's work as "ministering spirits, sent out to render service for the sake of those who will inherit eternal salvation" (Heb. 1:14), this does not mean they are privileged to know the full details of God's work or the recipients of His work (i.e., Christians).

> It is not unreasonable to suppose that there are many things in relation to the Divine character and plans, which they do not yet understand. They know, undoubtedly, much more than we do; but there are plans and purposes of God which are yet made known to none of his creatures. No one can doubt that these plans and purposes must be the object of the attentive study of all holy created minds … [Furthermore,] there are great and difficult questions about the whole subject of forgiveness, which an angel could easily see, but which he could not so easily solve. How could it be done consistently with the justice and truth of God? How could he forgive, and yet maintain the honour [*sic*] of his own law, and the stability of his own throne?[40]

---

39   I discuss this perspective in considerable detail in my book, *This World Is Not Your Home* (Spiritbuilding Publishers, 2022); go to www.spiritbuilding.com/chad.

40   Barnes, *Barnes' Notes* (electronic), on 1:12; bracketed word is mine.

There are many things we can speculate concerning angels and the angelic realm, to be sure. But we only know of their world what God has revealed to us, and they only know of our world what God has revealed to them. The One who knows *both* worlds perfectly, absolutely, and at any given moment, is God Himself. We would do well not to forget this.

A Holy People
(1 Peter 1:13 – 2:3)

The Need for Holiness (1:13–16): "Therefore"—since the preceding information is true—"prepare your minds for action" (1:13). The KJV translates this awkwardly: "gird up the loins of your mind." A man in the ancient world who is preparing to do some physical work would have to gather up his loose clothing and tie (or girdle) it around his thighs ("loins") to free up his legs for movement, traveling on a journey, running, or fighting (as in Exod. 12:11 or Eph. 6:14).[41] Modern equivalents to this metaphor would be to "roll up one's sleeves" or "take off one's coat." Peter here emphasizes the need for the believer to gather up his mental faculties to be ready to serve the One who promises him such a grand inheritance. Christians cannot be spectators or casual observers; they must roll up their sleeves, unencumber themselves of hindrances, and get busy to the task.

Being chosen by God for salvation always means there are things that the chosen must do. The **first** of these is to get their minds prepared to act in agreement with God's will. The **second** is to "keep [or, be] sober in spirit" (1:13)—lit., not be affected by strong drink; fig. (as Peter uses it), serious–minded, and thus attentive, watchful, vigilant, and not distracted by lesser things.[42] In essence, those who anticipate a heavenly inheritance with God ought not to allow their minds to be intoxicated with worldly things that would compromise this inheritance. The **third** is to "fix your hope" on God's grace, which means to put one's full trust, confidence, and faith in the One who secures his heavenly future.

41   Robertson, *Word Pictures* (electronic), on 1:13.

42   Vincent, *Word Studies* (electronic), on 1:13.

Grace can be defined as *everything* God does for the believer's salvation that he cannot do for himself. Thus, the believer does have things to do—this is what faithful obedience necessarily implies. But one substantial aspect of faith is to trust that God will in fact save the believer's soul. Human faith coupled with divine grace brings about a "new creature" (2 Cor. 5:17) and continues to be renewed day by day (2 Cor. 4:16, Eph. 4:22–24, Col. 3:9, etc.). The full realization of this grace—the time when all that God has done and has been doing—will be made visible when Christ Himself is made visible ("the revelation"). This can have no other reference in the NT than to His Second Coming.

The chosen of God have become (through spiritual adoption) sons of God, or simply "children" of God (or, God's children) (John 1:12–13, 1 John 3:1–3, Gal. 3:26–27, etc.).[43] Children are to be obedient, since this is the only right way to respond to their father's authority (Eph. 6:1). If we are to honor our physical parents here on earth, then how much more should spiritual children honor their Father who is in heaven? Thus, "as obedient children [or, children of obedience]," Christians have a moral responsibility to conduct themselves in a manner befitting their spiritual relationship with God (1:14).

Specifically, this conduct requires turning away from the "former lusts"—i.e., the self–serving, carnally–gratifying, and sensual pleasures of sin—and instead turning toward "the Holy One who called you" (1:15). (The language here is strongly reminiscent of Paul's words in Rom. 12:1–2.) "Conform" literally means "to pattern (oneself) with" a certain fashion, form, or expectation.[44] Carnal desires make us look like everyone else; Christ wants us to look like Him. A decision, then, must be made—not once, or occasionally, but continuously and even

---

43 On "obedient children," Guy N. Woods writes: "This phrase is a Hebraism, a form of expression often occurring in Hebrew and other Oriental languages, in which matters closely and intimately related are presented under the figure of the relationship which exists between a child and his parents. Thus, 'a child of obedience' is one who belongs to obedience and has partaken of its nature as a child belongs to, and has inherited the nature of, its parents" (*A Commentary on the New Testament Epistles of Peter, John, and Jude* [Nashville: Gospel Advocate Co., 1979], 39).

44 Strong, *Dictionary* (electronic), G4964.

aggressively, since the world does not want to let go of its prisoners. John's words (1 John 4:4–6) are especially relevant here:

> You are from God, little children, and have overcome them; because greater is He who is in you than he who is in the world. They [i.e., those who reject Jesus' divine nature—MY WORDS] are from the world; therefore they speak as from the world, and the world listens to them. We are from God; he who knows God listens to us; he who is not from God does not listen to us. By this we know the spirit of truth and the spirit of error.

Peter says that our "former lusts" were committed in ignorance (1:14; cf. Eph. 2:1–3 and Titus 3:1–3). We did not understand the full scope of what we were doing; or we did not care what damage our deeds did to ourselves or anyone else. The Jewish leaders also crucified Jesus for this same reason (Acts 3:17, 1 Cor. 2:6–8). But now that we have been enlightened with the gospel, we no longer are to live in ignorance but in knowledge, truth, and light. Now that we know God (to the extent that He has revealed Himself, and to the extent that we are able), we are expected to conform no longer to the inferior but are to ascend upward to the superior.

"Be [or, become] holy … in all your behavior" (1:15)—not just from time to time, or when in the company of Christians, or when anyone is looking, but in *all* things and at *all* times.[45] We have not been called by an unholy god—such as one would find in a pagan, man–made, or demonic religion—but by the Supreme Being who has created and now presides over all things. "Though all the peoples walk each in the name of his god, as for us, we will walk in the name of the LORD our God forever and ever" (Micah 4:5).[46]

---

45   "The meaning [in *Koine* Greek] is not 'become!' but 'be!'—i.e., be decisively, settle it once for all that you be holy" (Lenski, *Interpretation*, 56; bracketed words are mine).

46   "It is a great truth, that men everywhere will imitate the God whom they worship. They will form their character in accordance with his. They will regard what he does as right. They will attempt to rise no higher in virtue than the God whom they adore, and they will practice freely what he is supposed to do or approve. Hence, by knowing what are the characteristics of the gods which are worshiped by any people, we may form a

An excellent calling demands an excellent response. "You shall be holy, for I am holy" (1:16) is a quote from God Himself, taken from Lev. 11:44 (cf. Lev. 19:2 and 20:7). "Holy" [Greek, *hagios*] means sacred, set apart, saintly/sanctified, free from all unholiness or corruption.[47] Being holy does not only mean "Behave yourselves," although this, too, is certainly implied. Rather, it speaks to the core of the believer's desire to be wholly united in fellowship with his God. We cannot become divine beings, but we are invited—indeed, *expected*—to model our thinking, love, conduct, and perspective after the Divine Being who has delivered us from spiritual death and who owns our soul's salvation. "Therefore," Paul concurs, "be imitators of God, as beloved children; and walk in love, just as Christ also loved you ..." (Eph. 5:1–2a). Being "chosen of God" (recall 1:2), we no longer live for ourselves but for Him (Gal. 2:20). "God's purpose for those whom He calls is twofold: first, that they may do His will, or practice obedience, and second, that they may become like Him, or grow in holiness."[48]

Our Priceless Redemption (1:17–21): "If you address as Father ..." (1:17)—i.e., since you address Him as such, or seeing that you do so. Addressing God as an impartial judge of *all* men's work means that He will also judge *our* work as well, and that this should cause us to "conduct [ourselves] in fear." "Fear," in this context, does not mean we should be terrified of Him, but that we should live reverently and in holiness. Not only should God's impartial judgment motivate Christians to live reverently, but so should the priceless purchase of our souls (1:18). We have been redeemed—ransomed, purchased back (as a slave), or delivered—by something far more valuable than material wealth, which is "perishable" (susceptible to corruption or destruction). The incalculable value of our soul's redemption ought to produce in us obedience, holiness, and gratitude. Silver, gold, and the "futile [or, vain] way of life" all indicate that Peter has Gentiles in mind rather than Jews;

---

correct estimate of the character of the people themselves; and hence, as the God who is the object of the Christian's worship is perfectly holy, the character of his worshipers should also be holy" (Barnes, *Barnes' Notes* , on 1:16).

47   Strong, *Dictionary* (electronic), G40.

48   Stibbs, *TNTC*, 84.

such things are more associated with pagan idolatry in Peter's day than with Judaism.[49]

Now Peter discloses the priceless redemptive agent: "precious blood … the blood of Christ" (1:19). Blood is the most appropriate means of atonement since it represents the life of the one that is sacrificed for another (Lev. 17:10–11). We know that animal blood cannot atone for human sins (Heb. 10:4), but God has provided for us "a lamb unblemished and spotless" that most certainly *does* provide such atonement. The reference is, of course, to lambs selected for sacrifice under the Levitical system (see Lev. 22:17–24). Such lambs had to be flawless, otherwise they were unacceptable for sacrifice. But the blood of such animals—and the blood of Christ—is only applied, so to speak, to those who are in covenant with God through Christ.

"In Him," "in Christ," and all such similar phrases indicate a covenant relationship, as in Eph. 1:7: "In Him [Christ] we have redemption through His blood, the forgiveness of our trespasses, according to the riches of His grace." God owns the covenant and thus lays down its terms; Christ's blood gives *life* to this covenant, so that it serves both parties beneficially. When we agree to God's terms of salvation, we enter a covenant relationship with Him through grace (Jesus' blood) and faith (our baptism). Thus, through water and blood we are inducted, so to speak, into fellowship with God. Once we are "in Him," then—and *only* then—"the blood of Jesus His Son cleanses us from all sin" (1 John 1:7). His blood will not be applied to those outside of covenant; this is a special privilege of those who are "chosen" (recall 1:1).

Peter explains more about the supremacy of Christ's role—and thus, the supreme value of His blood—to underscore the value of our redemption (1:20a). Christ was not merely an *idea* in God's mind before the foundation (or, beginning) of the world; He was "foreknown" to the

---

49   "Peter is not interested in the varied traditions within paganism, nor primarily in its religious beliefs. He sees paganism rather as a unified whole, and more as a way of life than as a belief system. As a way of life, it stands in every respect contrary to the way of life required of the Christian communities…, and in fact constitutes a mortal threat to those communities" (Michaels, *WBC*, 64–65).

Father and enjoyed a pre-existence with Him.[50] (The NT teaching on this is solid and irrefutable; see John 1:1–3, 14, 8:58, 17:24, 1 Cor. 8:5–6, Col. 1:15–18, and Heb. 1:2–3, for example.) The plan for Christ to be "the Lamb of God who takes away the sin of the world" (John 1:29) was determined in the eternity prior to the Creation; this "eternal purpose" (Eph. 3:11) was agreed to by Christ and carried out in Him (2 Tim. 1:8–11).

Christ's sacrificial offering, then, was not an afterthought, or a means to fix a hole in God's plan; instead, Christ *was* the plan, and He carried out God's will fully and flawlessly (John 17:4). Accordingly, He "has appeared in these last times" for our sake (1:20b)—i.e., He has been revealed "in the flesh" to carry out this eternal plan of redemption (1 Tim. 3:16; see Titus 2:11–14, Heb. 9:26, and 1 John 3:5). The "last times" in this case refers to the Christian dispensation of time; there is no earthly dispensation after this, nor will there be any "time" once *this* dispensation is ended.

Because of Christ's ministry, self-sacrifice, and resurrection from the dead, we can *believe in God*—not just His existence, but His love, His plan, His forgiveness, and His promises (1:21). Just as God raised His Son from the dead and ushered Him into eternal glory (Phil. 2:8–11), so we have every reason to believe that we also are raised from our spiritual deadness and will look forward to eternal glory with Him. Our "faith and hope are in God" because Christ has provided the doctrinal foundation *of* such faith and hope in His resurrection (Acts 17:30–31).

---

50   Woods, for one, has a problem with this conclusion, thinking that it robs Adam and Eve of their free will. "If God had already devised a plan for the redemption of man from a sin which was certain to be committed, how could Adam and Eve have avoided its commission?" (*Commentary*, 47). Such reasoning is unnecessary and, in my opinion, presumptive. God's foreknowledge of human behavior, when left to itself in the *context* of free will, does not force that behavior to happen; it simply acknowledges that it *will* happen in due time. Similarly, God put Jesus into the midst of a generation of Jews who would become His executioners. In doing so, God did not make them put Jesus to death—even though He needed it to be done—but He knew what kind of people they were, and thus He knew that if He gave them opportunity to carry out such a deed, they would certainly do so (Acts 2:22–23).

A Fervent Love for the Brethren (1:22–25): Peter now makes a practical application: "obedience to the truth" ought to manifest itself in "a sincere love of the brethren" (1:22a). It is impossible to separate one's professed love for God from his love for God's people (1 John 4:20 – 5:2). Such love must be "sincere"—i.e., unfeigned, unhypocritical, and authentic (Rom. 12:9, 2 Cor. 6:6, 1 Tim. 1:5, etc.). A soul purified by the blood of Christ is expected to offer a pure love to those who are also purified, since they have all been made members of the same family of God. So then, Peter says, "fervently love one another from the heart" (1:22b)—the emphasis here being on the word *fervently*, which means intently, earnestly, and unceasingly (as in 1 Peter 4:8).[51] Do not just talk about such love, he implies, but *show* it—and do so generously and often. *Since* Christ has so loved us, we ought to love others; *as* Christ has loved us, we ought to love in like manner (John 13:34–35).[52]

As the price of our redemption is imperishable and life–giving, so the word of God is imperishable and "living and enduring" (1:23). (On "born again," see comments on 1:3.) The "word of God" does not mean the literal pages and ink of a Bible, but the spiritual message of God— His gospel. This word is "living and active" (Heb. 4:12), since it has the power to perform God's work upon the human heart (Rom. 1:16, 1 Cor. 1:18). This word is likened to a seed which carries within it a future life of a mature plant, but only once it encounters good soil. Similarly, as the living "seed" of God's word encounters an honest and obedient heart, it produces a spiritual life within that person that will continue beyond his earthly life.

There is no doubt that the Holy Spirit is directly involved with this "seed"—some think He *is* the "seed"—and that the work it (the seed) performs is unnatural to any earthly expectations and

---

51   Strong, *Dictionary* (electronic), G1619; see also Vincent, *Word Studies* (electronic), on 1:22.

52   "The Christian loves primarily those in Christ; secondarily, all who might be in Christ, namely, all men, as Christ as man died for all, and as he hopes that they, too, may become his Christian brethren" (Steiger, quoted in JFB, *Commentary* , on 1:22).

humanly impossible to duplicate.[53] This unnatural work involves the transformation of a person's soul through a death–and–rebirth process (see notes on 1:3)—something a mere book (i.e., the Bible) cannot do. Peter quotes from Isa. 40:6–8 to underscore his point: the visible, material, and even living things of this world are destined to perish, but God's word can never die and will never diminish in power (1:24–25a). "So, in a created order which is bound to pass away, it is God's word which offers men a confidence which is more secure and participation in life which is more abiding."[54] "And this is the word which was preached [lit., was preached as good news] to you" (1:25b)—the gospel of salvation through Jesus Christ can be ignored, maligned, misrepresented, etc., but it cannot be destroyed or lose its ability to transform a willing human heart.

Longing for God's Word (2:1–3): What should the believer's continued response be to this good news? First, there are things to "put aside" to receive it more fully; second, there must be a strong yearning for it—a desire like that of an infant longing for its mother's milk (2:1–3). "Warnings against evil attitudes and practices have no point if

---

53   Based on simple botany, for a seed to produce a plant and its fruit, the seed must first die to what it was originally: it can no longer remain a seed. This presents problems if we conclude that the word of God (or even the Holy Spirit!) must "die" to what it is now to produce a redeemed soul. But even Jesus had to die to what *He* was—a man of flesh and blood—to become the Savior of the world; likewise, a person must die to the world in order to become a child of God (John 12:23–25). But we must be careful with how far we press Peter's analogy. Theology does not have to follow the laws of botany precisely for it to work, otherwise, we could never believe in resurrection (because plants that die *never* come back to life). It is true that the word of God cannot bring about its desired potential until it encounters a sincere and willing heart (cf. Mat. 13:1–9, 18–23), but it cannot become anything less than what it is. The sinner dies to his allegiance to sin; truth never dies to accommodate the sinner. Likewise, the Holy Spirit *never* dies or changes in the least—He is a Divine Being—but works through the agency of the written message, human messengers, earthly circumstances, and whatever other means He chooses to use to bring about a suitable harvest for the Father. The Son of God died *as a Man* for the sinner; the Father cannot die *as God* for anyone. All said, it is necessary to view the "seed" as an analogy rather than as a literal transformation of either the word of God or the Spirit of God. Even so, the word of God does have a transforming effect on the human heart, and the heart that is so transformed will bring about much "fruit."

54   Stibbs, *TNTC*, 95.

nothing is provided to take their place."[55] The things that Peter says must be "put aside" include:

- malice—specifically, the desire to harm someone; generally (as used here), wickedness of any kind.[56]
- deceit—lit., to catch with bait; also translated "guile" (see 2:22; cf. John 1:47). In essence, this is any diversion from the truth or trapping someone with clever lies.[57]
- hypocrisy—lit., acting under a feigned pretense; suppression of one's true intent while professing something quite the opposite.[58]
- envy—similar to jealousy, this refers to one's dark desire for that which someone else possesses, which is often accompanied by other evil behaviors (Mat. 27:18).
- slander—lit., to defame or speak against someone's character, as in James 4:11. The Greek word itself is used only here and in 2 Cor. 12:20.[59]
- Peter adds "all" to cover *every form* of whatever is mentioned. Likewise, Jesus said, "be on your guard against *every form* of greed" (Luke 12:15, emphasis added)—not just one kind or another, but *all* of them.

"Like newborn babies" (2:2) literally refers to infants who are still being breastfed. But the implication here is to newly "born" converts—Peter has already used "born again" twice to depict one's conversion to the Christian faith. This calls to mind the zeal, excitement, and anticipation to learn more of God's word that is often seen in new converts. With this

---

55   Michaels, *WBC*, 91.

56   Strong, *Dictionary* (electronic), G2549.

57   Robertson, *Word Pictures* (electronic), on 2:1. "'Without guile' is, literally, 'unadulterated.' In ancient times milk was often adulterated with gypsum, a chalky–like substance to increase its volume, thus rendering it impure and contaminated. Such adulteration became a figure of the admixture of false doctrine with the pure word of God. Irenaeus, an early Christian writer, born between 120 and 140 AD, said of the heretics of his time, 'They mix gypsum with the milk, they taint the heavenly doctrine with the poison of their errors'" (Woods, *Commentary*, 55).

58   The words "hypocrisy," "envy," and "slander" in 2:1 are plural nouns in the best Greek texts—thus, hypocrisies, envies, and slanders.

59   Robertson, *Word Pictures* (electronic), on 2:1.

idea, Peter is saying that *all* Christians ought to have this kind of desire for the gospel message that saves souls.[60] The "pure milk of the word" also speaks of the uncorrupted and unadulterated message, as opposed to one that has been maligned by empty tradition, false teachers, and false religion.[61] Just as an infant grows through the substance and nutrients of its mother's milk, so the believer grows through the pure, heavenly truth of God's word. In this case, Peter speaks of "milk" as that which nurtures and increases growth.[62] "If you have tasted…" means, in fact, *since* one has tasted God's kindness, by the fact of his having been redeemed by the blood of Christ.

A People for God's Own Possession
(1 Peter 2:4–12)

A Holy Temple in the Lord (2:4–8): While many have rejected Jesus as the Christ/Son of God, including His own countrymen, we who

---

60   Case in point: I watched a video recently of people in China who were opening a box filled with Bibles sent to them from the United States. They eagerly tore away the packaging, and each person excitedly grabbed a Bible, and many of them kissed it, held it close to their chest with both arms, and wept openly. To them, this was a priceless gift, not something to lug from car to pew and back again. This kind of longing for God's word helps to bring Peter's words to life—at least it did for me.

61   The phrase "of the word" in the Greek here literally refers to a rational religion or spiritual worship, as used in Rom. 12:2. "There is no doubt that there is allusion to the gospel in its purest and most simple form, as adapted to be the nutriment of the new-born soul. Probably there are two ideas here; one, that the proper aliment of piety is simple truth; the other, that the truths which they were to desire were the more elementary truths of the gospel, such as would be adapted to those who were babes in knowledge" (Barnes, *Barnes' Notes*, on 2:2).

62   In other places (1 Cor. 3:2 and Heb. 5:13), "milk" is used in a negative contrast to solid food, as a primary diet of the new believer that should be replaced by something more substantive over time. There is no contradiction here since the different writers are using the same term for different reasons. Jesus did the same thing with leaven, for example: in one lesson, He used it positively (Mat. 13:33); in another, negatively (Mat. 16:6).

believe in Him and His power to save us come to Him for what He has to offer *and* because He is worthy of our adoration (see John 6:66–69). He is in fact a "living stone," the cornerstone of God's spiritual temple.[63] Though Christ was rejected by men, He is "precious" to God (2:4b), being His only "beloved Son" (Col. 1:13; cf. John 3:16, "begotten Son"). "Choice" implies having been chosen, since no one else could fulfill what had to be done to bring sinful men back to God (reminiscent of Rev. 5:1–8). This choice provides the bedrock for all believers of all time and carries into eternity.

Thus, even before the world was made, the *decision* was made for Christ to be the foundation of human redemption after we fell from our innocence. A "living stone" is, of course, a paradox: stones are non–living things, yet Christ is very much alive; living beings never become stones, and stones never become alive. But in the spiritual context, this is not only possible, but it works beautifully.

Believers who are "chosen" and "born again" are not simply to revel in their newfound status. Rather, we have *come* to Christ and have become part of something far greater than ourselves—in effect, as participants in a grand, spiritual temple of God (2:4a; see Eph. 2:19–22 and Rev. 3:12).[64] The idea here is not only that of contributing to this spiritual temple, but also serving as living *witnesses* (or, testifiers of the facts) to men for God. (It was for this reason that stones were often used or erected; see Josh. 4:1–9 and 24:25–27, for example.) Christians are part of a spiritual "house"—"the greater and more perfect tabernacle, not made with hands, that is to say, not of this creation" (Heb. 9:11). We are also a "holy priesthood" (2:5) that alludes to the ancient Levitical priesthood but in fact has surpassed it in many respects.[65]

---

63 "Though Peter was himself a stone (*petros*), he was wholly unlike the stone (*lithos*) which he describes here. *Petros* is a fragment of native rock, unhewn; whereas, *lithos* is one shaped and fitted for the purpose designated" (Woods, *Commentary*, 57).

64 "Coming" is from "the compound verb *proserchesthai,* together with the repeated preposition *pros,* 'to whom' or 'towards whom,' [and] expresses the idea of drawing near with intention both to stay and to enjoy personal fellowship. The word is used in the LXX [i.e., Septuagint, or Greek translation of the OT] of drawing near to God in worship, to offer prayer and sacrifice" (Stibbs, *TNTC*, 98; bracketed words are mine).

65 "Peter does not urge, 'Be such stones, such a house, such a priesthood!' He

Priests are ministers to the God whom they worship; they offer sacrifices, carry out ministerial responsibilities, and set a holy example for others to follow. While the Levitical priests offered bloody sacrifices of animals, our sacrifice—the Lamb of God—was offered "once for all" (Heb. 10:10) and no blood sacrifices are required of Christians. Anyone who is in Christ can offer spiritual sacrifices—love, worship, praise, prayers, songs, service, hospitality, etc. (A priesthood–layman, or clergy–laity, system is foreign to the NT pattern.)

Peter now returns to speaking of Christ (the "living stone") as One who has fulfilled the prophecies concerning Him (2:6–8). The first prophecy ("Behold, I lay in Zion a choice stone …") is from Isa. 28:16, but is also used in Rom. 9:33, 10:11, and (in essence) Eph. 2:20. The second prophecy ("The stone which the builders rejected …") is from Psalm 118:22 but is also quoted by Jesus (Mat. 21:42). The third prophecy ("A stone of stumbling…") is from Isa. 8:14 and is inserted in Paul's own quotation of this prophecy in Rom. 9:33. "Zion," in messianic prophecies, implies "Christ's church" (see Isa. 4:2–5 and Heb. 12:22, for example).

A cornerstone is the largest and most important stone of the foundation of a building.[66] It not only sets the levelness of the structure, but also its stability and orientation; the integrity of the entire structure depends upon it being set properly. Until relatively recent times, cornerstones were set amidst ceremonies and celebrations, in anticipation of the great building which would be established upon it. Likewise, Christ is the principal foundation of His holy church, the ancient prophets and NT apostles being the rest of that foundation (Eph. 2:20). So solid, permanent, and indestructible is this cornerstone, whoever "believes in Him will not be disappointed" (2:6). To "believe" here means to

---

declares that we *are* all of this. This means that he now sets forth the basis on which the preceding hortations [i.e., strong urgings or appeals, specifically those in 1:13 – 2:3] rest" (Lenski, *Interpretation*, 82; bracketed words are mine).

66   In some cases, a cornerstone refers to the capstone in the highest part of a stone arch. The way Peter uses the imagery, however, clearly refers to a foundational stone. This is what is meant in the passage he cites (Isa. 28:16) and is consistent with Paul's own imagery (Eph. 2:20).

obey (John 3:36). "Disappointed" can also be rendered "put to shame," "disgraced," or "humiliated."[67] The meaning is: no one will have any regrets for having put his full confidence in the Lord Jesus Christ, since He is "faithful and true" (Rev. 3:14) to keep His promises of salvation.

The precious cornerstone is only of benefit to those who believe, not to those who refuse to believe (for any reason) (2:7).[68] Most of Jesus' own countrymen (the Jews) rejected His role as the Messiah/Christ and His identity as the Son of God (John 1:10–11). This rejection did not result in salvation, but condemnation.

> In the quotation from Psalm 118:22, the psalmist borrows a figure from the building trade. Stones used in the construction of buildings had to be regular in size. They were cut with the aid of a hammer or a chisel or even a saw (1 Kings 7:9). Stones that did not pass inspection were rejected by the builders. The builders figuratively represent the unbelievers who reject the stone that is Christ. God, the chief architect, takes this reject and puts it down as capstone. He honors Christ by giving him the preeminent position in the building, that is, God's household.[69]

To "stumble," in this context, means to sin; the specific sin here is that of disbelief, despite all the proofs, evidence, and eyewitnesses that God had provided to the contrary (2:8). A "rock of offense" means that they sinned *against* the "rock," not that the rock *caused* their sin. When people reject the gospel, the gospel no longer works to save them but condemns them; likewise, when people reject Christ, He does not become their Savior but their Judge. Their disobedience to "the word"—the divinely–revealed message of God, as spoken through His Son (Heb. 1:1–2, 2:3–4)—results in their "doom."

---

67 *NASB Greek-Hebrew Dictionary*, electronic edition (Robert L. Thomas and W. Don Wilkins, gen. eds.; © 1981, 1998 by the Lockman Foundation), G2617b.

68 The "corner {stone}" or (KJV) "head of the corner" refer to the same thing—the foundational cornerstone (Clowney, *Message*, 85).

69 Kistemaker, *NTC*, 89.

As it was for them, so it will be for every other person who refuses to believe in all the evidence God has provided concerning His Son. An "appointed" doom is no different than being "chosen" for salvation: it refers to the group, not the individual. All those who believe will be saved; all those who disbelieve will be condemned (Mark 16:15–16). In either case, the decision to be saved or condemned rests upon the individual person's response to the gospel message, not upon God alone. The preaching of the gospel—by Christ, the apostles, or us—is rendered completely useless if God has already decided who will be saved or lost.

Those Who Are Called (2:9–12): Instead of dwelling upon the doom of unbelievers, Peter turns to the positive characteristics of Christ's church (the collective "you") (2:9–10). The descriptors he uses here are all derived from the OT: "a chosen race [or, people]" (Deut. 10:15); "a royal priesthood" (Isa. 61:6); "a holy nation" (Exod. 19:6); and "a people for God's own possession" (Exod. 19:5, Deut. 4:20; cf. Titus 2:14).

While Christ's church is comparable to the nation of Israel, significant differences remain. **First,** Israel's covenant with God was national; ours is on an individual basis. **Second,** Israel's priesthood, sacrificial system, and tabernacle were physical; ours is spiritual. **Third,** the entire Levitical system was incomplete, and anticipated a fulfillment outside of itself; our system is entirely fulfilled in Christ. **Fourth,** Israel's inheritance was directly tied to the land; our inheritance (or "citizenship") is in heaven (Phil. 3:20–21). (Other contrasts remain, though we will not pursue them here.) We *collectively*, as the church universal, are designated in much the same way Israel was, but everything about the church transcends the nation of Israel because of what Christ has accomplished.[70]

"So that you may proclaim the excellencies" of God indicates a divine *purpose* for His people upon the earth (2:9b). God deserves to be

---

70 Lenski makes a good point: if Christians are a priesthood, then there can be no human agency that stands between us and God—no man, body of men, church, religion, or tradition (*Interpretation,* 100). Christ is our only mediator (1 Tim. 2:5), and through Him we have full and confident access to the Father (Heb. 10:19–22).

praised simply because He is our Creator, the source of all that exists
(Rev. 4:11); He also deserves to be praised for His goodness, virtue, and
holiness. Those most fit to praise Him are faithful Christians since they
are in fellowship with Him and therefore have tasted of His kindness
(recall 2:1–3). These also have been called "out of darkness" through the
gospel "into His marvelous light." The "domain of darkness" (Col. 1:13)
is the realm of Satan, demons, wickedness, and all that is unholy—a
realm to which we once belonged (Eph. 2:1–3).

God's world is characterized by light—knowledge, goodness, purity,
and holiness. God Himself is Light (1 John 1:5), and those who walk
in fellowship with Him also walk in light. His light is "marvelous" (or,
wonderful), pure (James 1:17), and—to us who remain in our earthly
state—"unapproachable" (1 Tim. 6:16). Peter quotes from the prophet
Hosea to show that the universal *church*—not the literal nation of
Israel—is the fulfillment of such prophecies (2:10; see Hos. 1:10 and
2:23). Those who once were outside of God's covenant with Israel
(Eph. 2:13–18, 4:17–19) are now invited into a new covenant that is
not dependent upon animal sacrifices, a human priesthood, or human
genealogy, but rests upon the blood and priesthood of Jesus Christ.[71]

Those who have been called, sprinkled with blood, sanctified by the
Spirit of God, and shown mercy have a moral responsibility to live in
a manner worthy of their calling (2:11–12; see Eph. 4:1). On "aliens"
(or, "foreigners") and "strangers" (or, "sojourners"; "pilgrims"), see
comments on 1:1. Foreigners are those who do not belong; sojourners
are those who are passing through. Both describe the Christian's spiritual
relationship to the world of the unconverted: we do not belong to it any
longer, and we are simply on our way to somewhere else.[72]

---

71 "Peter uses the terminology to remind his Gentile readers that they are Gentiles.
They were not always the people of God but have become so by God's mercy now
revealed in Jesus Christ" (Michaels, *WBC*, 112). Even so, Hosea's prophecy was
directed toward *Israelites*, to remind *them* that they also are only God's people because
of His mercy and grace, and not because of their own merit.

72 "In any museum we will find quite ordinary things—clothes, a walking–stick,
a pen, books, pieces of furniture—which are only of value because they were once
possessed and used by some great person. It is the ownership which gives them worth.

Even so, "fleshly lusts" (or, "carnal desires") still exert a strong pull on our human nature, often creating a vicious conflict between our desire to serve God and the desire to gratify carnal appetites (Gal. 5:16–17). While we are to "make no provision for the flesh with regard to its lusts" (Rom. 13:14), this does not mean that such lusts merely evaporate and lose all seductive influence. On the other hand, it *does* mean that we can choose not to listen to their siren call. The important thing to remember here is that there *is* a war that rages within—an unseen but very real struggle—and only one side or the other will win. We want to do well, but we are being unrelentingly assaulted with wicked desires "of the flesh" (Gal. 5:19–21).[73] With this in mind, the believer should:

❑ Not regard this world as his home; he seeks a far better "city" than whatever is found here (Heb. 11:13–16).
❑ Regard his earthly life as temporary and transient, not permanent and fixed.
❑ Not allow any earthly circumstance, relationship, or commitment to compromise his heavenward journey.
❑ Keep his heart and focus fixed intently upon where he is going, not on this present world (Mat. 6:33, 2 Cor. 4:16–18, Col. 3:1–4, and Heb. 12:1–3).
❑ Not burden himself with worldly possessions, wealth, or attachments—things that will make the journey far more difficult, not less. Those who are traveling will pack lightly, knowing that they need only what is necessary, not that which gives only temporary joy.
❑ Not only fight against carnal desires, but also put them to death (Rom. 8:13). In other words, our struggle with the flesh is not a gentleman's disagreement or passive conflict, but is visceral, bloody, and brutal. We are not merely slapping our opponent (i.e., wicked behaviors) in the face with a white glove, as though this were a gentlemanly dispute; we are seeking to kill it.

It is so with the Christian. The Christian may be a very ordinary person, but he acquires a new value and dignity and greatness because he belongs to God. The greatness of the Christian lies in the fact that he is God's" (Barclay, *Letters*, 236).

73   "The regenerated soul is besieged by sinful lusts. Like Samson in the lap of Delilah, the believer, the moment that he gives way to fleshly lusts, has the locks of his strength shorn, and ceases to maintain that spiritual separation from the world and the flesh of which the Nazarite vow was the type" (JFB, *Commentary*, on 2:11).

"Keep your behavior excellent among the Gentiles" (2:12)—i.e., among unconverted men (as "Gentiles" is also used in 3 John 1:7). Such ungodly and spiritually ignorant people are always looking for a way to discredit and accuse godly people with a failure to uphold their professed religion. The early church, for example, was accused of cannibalism (by eating the Lord's Supper), undermining the secular economy (by turning people away from supporting idolatry, as in Acts 19:23ff), inciting rebellion (by allegedly fomenting the revolt of slaves against their masters), a general hatred of mankind (because they separated themselves from "the world"), and rebellion to Caesar (because they gave their allegiance to the Lord).[74]

Even when believers walk with God, they will be seen among ungodly men as troublemakers (Acts 24:5), criminals (Acts 18:13), and those who deserve to be killed (Rev. 11:7–10). Thus, faithful Christians will be slandered by wicked people—and yet, Peter says, the wicked will have no real grounds for such reproach. Their accusations will be baseless and unprovable, whereas the godly person's deeds will vindicate him in the end. The word "observe" here means to view or inspect with scrutiny.[75] In other words, the unconverted observer's initial view of Christians may be, due to ignorance or prejudice, a very negative and condemning one; yet, upon close inspection, he will have no good reason to maintain such an assessment as he sees the believer's noble and virtuous conduct over time. Instead of condemning the believer, the unbeliever may himself become a Christian and "glorify God" rather than remaining separated from Him.

"In the day of visitation" (2:12) is variously interpreted as:

❑ God's "visitation" of mercy upon the sinner at the time of his conversion.
❑ a specific time of persecution (e.g., the destruction of Jerusalem in AD 70).
❑ a general or unspecified time of persecution.

---

74 Adapted from Barclay, *Letters*, 240–1.

75 Strong, *Dictionary* (electronic), G2029.

- the Second Coming of Christ.
- Judgment Day.

This "day" is obviously something in which God "visits" men, whether for salvation or judgment. Since "every knee will bow" at their presentation before Christ (Phil. 2:9–10), some think that this will be the time of glorification of which Peter speaks. The context, however, leaves us with the strong impression that this is a *favorable* visitation, not one involving judgment. The faithful believer's good conduct in the presence of his enemies will cause them to reconsider their wickedness, possibly turn their hearts to God, and give Him glory as a result. This seems the most natural and logical conclusion here.

A General Call to Submission
(1 Peter 2:13–25)

Various Contexts of Submission (2:13–17): The concept of submission is largely misunderstood among both Christians and non–Christians alike. "Submit" (2:13) in the Greek [*hupotasso*] literally means "to subordinate [oneself]; to put oneself under [the authority of] someone else."[76] It is variously translated in the NT as: "put under," "be subject to," "submit [oneself] to," "be in subjection to," and similar expressions. The meaning is always that of a *voluntary* decision to yield oneself to another person or higher power. For example, it is not the "human institution" that is to force subjection upon the people, but Christians are to submit themselves to human institutions. This is the case of a wife to her husband (Eph. 5:22), Christians to other Christians (Eph. 5:21), Christians toward those who labor extensively in the brotherhood (1 Cor. 16:15–16), the church to Christ (Eph. 5:24), angels to Christ (1 Pet. 3:22), and even Christ to the Father (1 Cor. 15:27–28).

---

76   *Ibid.*, G5293; bracketed words are mine.

But this is not how everyone sees "submission." Today, submission has become a kind of dirty word—a term implying slavery, oppression, injustice, forced constraints, and an imposition upon one's personal freedom. While it is true that relationships involving submission can be and are abused (most commonly, in marriage), this does not render the idea wicked or unjust. For there to be civil peace, there must be those in authority and those who voluntarily submit to that authority. For relationships to work as God intended, there must be those who are respected and those who give such respect. (In the brotherhood, this regularly goes both ways, as in Eph. 5:21 and Phil. 2:2–3.)

To submit to human institutions, then, is necessary—for several reasons. **First,** governing authority ultimately derives its power from and is established by God Himself; to resist that authority unnecessarily is to resist God (Rom. 13:1–4). **Second,** God is not a God of confusion or disorder, but of peace and stability (1 Cor. 14:33, 40); for these to exist, there must be law and order, and thus there must be lawmakers and law-keepers. **Third,** "rebellion is as the sin of divination, and insubordination is as iniquity and idolatry" (1 Sam. 15:23a); God does not want His people involved with or being identified as rebels, since this puts Him *and* them in a very bad light. "For the Lord's sake" (2:13) involves all three of the reasons offered here.[77]

"Every human institution [or, human authority; ordinance of man; human creation]" refers to any legal government that presides over men for the purpose of keeping law and order (2:13–14). Such governments

---

77 It is likely, too, that Peter wrote this to counter any claims among Christians that, since they answered directly to God, they no longer had to answer to men. Peter's own statement in Acts 5:29 ("We must obey God rather than men") might have been misconstrued to mean this. While his was indeed correct, it cannot be universally applied to any and every situation. Peter and the apostles were not in willful rebellion to Jewish authority; they were simply carrying out what they were commissioned to do by Christ. Only when these two authorities contradicted each other (as in Acts 5:28) did Peter appeal to the *higher* command of God "rather than" that of mere men. It would be wrong, therefore, to apply Peter's words to a Christian's relationship to his secular government in times of peace, in the absence of religious persecution, and in all cases where he is not forced *by* that government to violate his conscience or God's doctrine.

are created by men but are provided by God. (This is meant generally. In other words, God does not "provide" an evil government, but He does provide human authority to govern men. The fact that men abuse governing powers does not invalidate the initial purpose *for* those powers.) Whether dealing with the entire institution of government, or the individual representatives of that government ("king" or "governors"), the Christian is called by God to be submissive and obedient. Governors are those who serve as an extension of the king's power; they are "sent by him [i.e., the king]" either for punishment or praise, depending on citizens' responses to their authority. "The only justifiable exception is in cases where obedience to the earthly king plainly involves disobedience to the express command of the King of kings."[78]

The Christian's submissive posture is "for the Lord's sake" (recall 2:13) and "the will of God" (2:15). God expects His people to do what is right, even to their own hurt (as Peter will expound upon shortly). Rebellion, retaliation, vengeance, and self–vindication are what we expect from ungodly and unconverted people; submission, compliance, obedience, and allowing *God* to vindicate is what we should expect from faithful Christians. This will "silence" [lit., muzzle; render speechless] those who think and live otherwise.[79] Wise men listen to God and follow Him; ignorant and foolish men think for themselves and follow their carnal desires or human emotions. When foolish men are confronted with noble Christian behavior, they may be convinced that there is something *greater than men* which should compel them to act. Rather than simply opening their mouths to ridicule or denounce, they might open their eyes, their ears, and their hearts to the truth.

"Act as free men" (2:16)—in other words, live as those who are free to choose one thing over another, but be wise to choose what is *right*

---

78 JFB, *Commentary* (electronic), on 2:14.

79 "The same verb [Greek, *phimoun*; G5392] is used to express what our Lord did when He 'put the Sadducees to silence' (Mat. 22:34); and what He said when He silenced an unclean spirit (Mark 1:25), and when He stilled the storm (Mark 4:39). The word can cover the idea of preventing someone from speaking, as well as the idea of causing someone to cease from speaking" (Stibbs, *TNTC*, 111; bracketed words are mine).

rather than what is *wrong*. The Jews considered themselves free men (see John 8:33), but they also acted wickedly toward Jesus and held the Roman government in contempt. While the Christian has the freedom *in Christ* to exercise his faith and his conscience, he does not have the freedom to use these as an excuse to do what is evil (as in, "I don't have to obey human government, since my allegiance is solely to Christ!"). As "bondslaves of God," we are to represent Him rightly and never cast His name in an ugly light through our own poor behavior.

In summary, "Honor all people, love the brotherhood, fear God, honor the king" (2:17)—a powerful and significant statement, to be sure. To "honor" someone means to treat them with dignity, value, and respect. "All people" is not limited to any one group, but because of the following phrase ("the brotherhood"), Peter obviously has unbelievers in mind. We are to honor *all* people, whether: we personally agree with them; they are friends or enemies (Mat. 5:44, Luke 6:27); they are our masters or our servants (Eph. 6:9, 1 Tim. 6:1); they are above us (as governing authorities) or below us (as subordinates to our own secular authority). "The brotherhood [or, the brethren]" refers exclusively to those who are in Christ. We are all "brothers" because of a common faith, but also because we are all "sons of God" (Gal. 3:26) and therefore heirs of a heavenly inheritance.

To "fear God" means to defer to His authority and show Him reverence for the divine being that He is. To fear God is the first principle of the Christian faith since no profession of faith is worth anything until God is honored and respected above all else. "Honor the king" means to value and respect the position and authority of those who oversee the nation. Not only are we to honor the king, but we are also to pray for him; and "This is good and acceptable in the sight of God our Savior" (1 Tim. 2:1–3). By extension, Christians are to honor their mayor, governor, and president—whether we voted for him, agree with him, or subscribe to his political party. It is unchristian–like to show open contempt for secular rulers.

The world watches to see how we will conduct ourselves, even in the case of social, political, and even religious disagreement. When we act no differently than ungodly people act, we fail to represent our God rightly *to* such people. "If religion fails there [i.e., in the public arena], they judge that it fails altogether; and however devout we may be in private, if it is not seen by the world that our religion leads to the faithful performance of the duties which we owe in the various relations of life, it will be regarded as of little value."[80]

Servants and Masters (2:18–20): Peter now turns his attention to the servant–master relationship (2:18). "Servants" [Greek, *oiketes*] refers specifically here to servants of the home/house, yet in principle extends to slaves of any kind.[81] This is an important command, since slaves comprised a healthy percentage of the Roman Empire's overall population.[82] Likewise, many early Christians were slaves, since the gospel's message of redemption, deliverance, and hope especially appealed to them. Just because a slave becomes a Christian, however, does not nullify his loyalty to his master. Quite the opposite: the relationship ought to improve, as far as the servant's attitude is concerned. He has no right, Peter implies, to assume that his newfound freedom in Christ gives him freedom from his earthly responsibilities or restraints. Paul's words are also helpful here (Col. 3:22–25):

> Masters, grant to your slaves justice and fairness, knowing that you too have a Master in heaven (Eph. 6:9). Slaves, in all things obey those who are your masters on earth, not with external service, as those who merely please men, but with sincerity of heart, fearing the Lord. Whatever you do, do your work heartily,

---

80   Barnes, *Barnes' Notes* (electronic), on 2:17; bracketed words are mine.

81   Robertson, *Word Pictures* (electronic), on 2:18.

82   There were an estimated 60,000,000 slaves in the Roman Empire during Peter's lifetime. Not all slaves were manual laborers; some were doctors, teachers, musicians, actors, secretaries, and stewards. Many people became slaves through circumstances out of their control (i.e., conquest of their nation, prisoners of war, being born into slavery, etc.); others chose to become slaves because they had no other means by which to support themselves. Some slaves were loved by their masters, treated as members of the family, and respected. In many other cases, however, the slave was regarded *by law* as a thing without legal rights, not dignified as a human being. In such cases, men and women alike were treated like mere possessions, on the level of cattle, and were expendable (adapted from Barclay, *Letters*, 247, 249–50).

as for the Lord rather than for men, knowing that from the Lord you will receive the reward of the inheritance. It is the Lord Christ whom you serve. For he who does wrong will receive the consequences of the wrong which he has done, and that without partiality.

Servants/slaves are to "be submissive…with all respect" (2:18)—i.e., not with false respect, false loyalty, or only when the master is looking. Paul again helps us: "Slaves, be obedient to those who are your masters according to the flesh, with fear and trembling, in the sincerity of your heart, as to Christ; not by way of eyeservice, as men-pleasers, but as slaves of Christ, doing the will of God from the heart" (Eph. 6:5–6). Such submission/service is not to be offered only under ideal circumstances, that is, for "good and gentle" masters, but in all cases. "Unreasonable" is from the Greek word *skolios* (from which we get "scoliosis," crookedness of the spine), and means crooked, perverse, untoward, or (morally) warped.[83] Some masters are good men; others are wicked men; servants are to serve both kinds of men with equal loyalty and respect.

The unspoken question here is, "Why?" Peter answers this immediately: "For this finds favor" with God, since He does not expect His servants to be submissive only when it is comfortable and convenient, but even when it is uncomfortable and to their own hurt (2:19).[84] "For the sake of conscience" indicates that such a servant believes what he is doing (in bearing "up under sorrows when suffering unjustly") meets God's approval, and is striving to please Him. This may seem to be a lot to ask of someone who—being a slave of another man—is already in a position of disadvantage. But God sees things differently: righteous behavior must not be dependent upon or conditioned by circumstances. One's station in life is irrelevant in this case; God would expect the same of a

---

83   Strong, *Dictionary* (electronic), G4646.

84   "Favor" (2:19 and 2:20) is from the Greek *charis*, and is most often translated "grace" in the NT. Using the word "grace" here, however, makes for an awkward and unclear reading ("For this finds grace …"). The context clearly communicates the idea of seeking God's *approval*, and thus "favor" removes all problems.

master, rich man, or king, if indeed that man belonged to Him.

However, if a person is suffering or being "harshly treated" because of his own sin, that is a different matter altogether (2:20). That man gets what he deserves; there is no honor in his suffering, since he is not suffering for doing what is *right* but for what is *wrong*. (Imagine, for example, a Christian slave who is punished for stealing something from his master. His crime forfeits any "favor," even if he endures his punishment with patience.) But patient endurance of unjust suffering for what is *right* finds "favor with God." Peter could not be clearer on this subject.

Christ's Model Example (2:21–25): The need to do what is right even to one's own hurt is not limited to slaves, however. Peter applies this principle to *all* believers, and then cites Christ as our ultimate example (2:21–24).[85] Christ taught us **first** that *He* must suffer in His role as the Servant of God, the personification of Israel (Isa. 50:6, 53:1–12, Luke 24:25–27, etc.); **second,** that His suffering would be for others (Mark 10:45); and **third,** that all who follow Him must also suffer.[86] In fact, Christians are "called *for this purpose*" (2:21, emphasis added): this is not an afterthought but is part of God's original intention for us. Likewise, the fact that Christ suffered unjustly as the world's redeemer is a matter of prophecy and historical record (see Mat. 16:21, Acts 17:2–3, and 26:22–23). He is not asking Christians to do anything that He has not already done; in fact, none of us will ever suffer as much as He did for doing what is right.

---

85   The Greek word (*hypogrammos*) for the English word "example" is used only here in the NT. It refers to something written down that is supposed to be traced or copied by someone else, as when alphabet letters are written on a page and then copied by a child who is learning that alphabet (Robertson, *Word Pictures*, on 2:21). In a very real sense, Christ has written down (through the inspiration of the Holy Spirit) exactly what we are to follow; we are to trace the steps that He already walked (1 John 2:6).

86   In this passage (2:21–25), there are several allusions to OT Scripture, particularly Isa. 53. This, and the several other places where Peter draws on OT passages (including his speeches or sermons in Acts 2 – 5), reminds us of what Jesus said to him and the other disciples: "'These are My words which I spoke to you while I was still with you, that all things which are written about Me in the Law of Moses and the Prophets and the Psalms must be fulfilled.' Then He opened their minds to understand the Scriptures…" (Luke 24:44–45).

While we may well suffer the consequences of our own sins, Christ deserved no such suffering since He committed no sin (2:22; see Isa. 53:9). He was perfectly holy and just; He is the only Man who is literally justified by law, since He never violated God's law even once. Not only did He commit no sin in His behavior, but His heart was pure and holy, and the measurement of one's heart is what comes out of his mouth (Mat. 15:17–19, James 1:26, 3:2, etc.). Christ always spoke truthfully, factually, and accurately; he never spoke with hypocrisy, insincerity, or the intention to deceive anyone. Even when He was "reviled [lit., vilified or abused with words]," He did not respond in like manner, nor did He try to vindicate Himself (2:23). Even when He suffered personal shame, injury, and pain, He did not attempt to defend Himself or counterattack. Instead, He "kept entrusting Himself to Him who judges righteously"— i.e., Christ did not seek justice among unrighteous men but knew His Father would justify Him. Christ was patient to wait for that time in which He would be exonerated—as indeed He was (Phil. 2:8–11).

While we can follow His example of suffering (in our own circumstances), Christ went above and beyond what we can do (2:24a). He "bore our sins in His body on the cross [or, carried our sins in His body up to the cross]," an allusion to placing a sacrificial animal upon an altar.[87] This was something we could not do for ourselves or anyone else, nor could anyone else do this for us (Isa. 53:4, 12). This suffering was extremely personal ("in His body"): He did not merely talk about suffering, conceptualize His suffering, or promise to suffer if necessary (but then sought to avoid it). Rather, He personally and painfully endured the suffering of crucifixion—and all the other unspeakable horrors that dying for the sins of the world brought upon Him—to redeem those who believe in Him.

Such was Christ's part in our redemption. Our part is to "die to sin and live to righteousness" (2:24b). This does not—in fact, cannot—mean that we are rendered insensitive to temptation and therefore unable to

---

87   The word for "cross" here is from Greek, *xulon* ("tree"), the same word Peter used in his sermons (Acts 5:30 and 10:39), and what Paul also used (Gal. 3:13), both men likely influenced by Deut. 21:23 (Woods, *Commentary*, 83).

sin anymore. Rather, it means that our allegiance has changed: we no longer serve sin as our master, but we have chosen instead to serve a new Master—paradoxically, the One who has died for us on the cross (Rom. 6:11–18). As we have chosen to separate ourselves from the world and its sin, so we must also choose to join ourselves to Christ in righteousness (2 Cor. 6:14 – 7:1, Gal. 2:20); these are mutually–dependent states of being.

"For by His wounds you were healed"—"wounds [or, stripes]" here involves the entirety of Christ's ordeal as an offering for sin. He was wounded *so that* we would be "healed" (i.e., forgiven, restored to fellowship, and given life in place of death; cf. Isa. 53:5). It should be noted that animals offered for sacrifice were never *punished* or *tortured* first but were treated with dignity and respect. Our Lord, however, was ridiculed with great contempt, received barbaric treatment, and was subjected to unspeakable humiliation. He suffered *as though* He were guilty yet was innocent. God does not punish the innocent, but He does allow the innocent—even His own Son—to suffer for the sake of righteousness. God allowed His Son to *die* in our place, but He did not *punish* Him in our place. It was men who inflicted the welts, bruises, and stripes (whipping marks) upon our Lord; it was men who punched Him, spit upon Him, and pressed a crown of thorns to His head; and it was men who nailed Him to a cross to die. God allowed these things to happen, but it was men who *made* them happen.

Prior to becoming Christians, we were lost, morally confused, and "continually straying like sheep" without a shepherd (2:25; see Isa. 53:6, Mat. 9:36). In that directionless and vulnerable state of being, we were exposed to and unprotected from the world's lies, deceit, and corruption. But Christ has given us light instead of darkness, truth instead of ignorance, and order instead of chaos. He is the good Shepherd who seeks to reclaim for God what was lost through the deception of sin (Luke 19:10, John 10:11). His leadership guides us to where we need to be; His guardianship protects us from being destroyed by our "adversary, the devil" (1 Peter 5:8; see John 10:27–29); "We are His people and the sheep of His pasture" (Psalm 100:3).

"Guardian" [Greek, *episkopos*] is the same word rendered "bishop" or "overseer" elsewhere in the NT (as in Acts 20:28) with reference to church elders. Christ is the "Chief Shepherd" (1 Peter 5:4) of the redeemed; therefore, "He is the head of His body, the church" (Col. 1:18). "Of your souls" indicates the spiritual nature of His oversight of the church, although it is true that He oversees the physical world as well, as He is the creator and sustainer of all things (Col. 1:16–17).

Submission in Marriage
(1 Peter 3:1–7)

Wives' Submission to their Husbands (3:1–6): "In the same way [or, In like manner]" (3:1a) connects with what has just been said: believers must be willing to serve the Savior and therefore suffer for what is right, even in the marriage relationship, even when the situation is unfair. "You wives" refers to Christians who *are* wives; Peter addresses these women directly here. "Your own husbands" refers not to *other* wives' husbands, but only their own. "Submissive" carries all the meaning and implications as Peter instructed earlier (recall 2:13, 18). This is to be the case whether one's husband is a believer (faithful Christian) or yet "disobedient to the word" of God.

The natural explanation here is that of a wife who has obeyed the gospel, but her husband has not. This unequally yoked situation would inevitably create conflicts, which is the reason for Peter's instructions here. Under Roman law, a woman had no rights of her own; while she remained at home, she was under the "law" of her father; when she married, she was given to her husband under this same circumstance. Our 21st century American perspective—namely, that women can allegedly live independently of their husbands—must not be pressed upon the context here.

In the middle of the first century, a wife was expected to profess the religion of her husband. If the husband adopted the Christian faith, his spouse would have to do so, too. But if the wife became a Christian, her husband would [or, might] consider her unfaithful to him and his pagan religion. This caused tension in the home. Peter therefore counsels these wives to submit to their spouses, even if their husbands make life miserable for them because of their Christian commitment. He fully realizes the predicament of Christian women whose husbands refuse to listen to the gospel.[88]

It is difficult for us to imagine the courage of a woman (in Peter's day) to choose to follow Christ when her husband did not.[89]

"They may be won ..." (3:1b)—that is, to the Lord. The "behavior of their wives" will, in such cases, show the excellent value of the gospel as demonstrated through the "chaste and respectful behavior" of their wives (3:2). "Chaste" is translated from the same Greek root word as used for "holy"; here, it means modest, pure, (morally) clean, or blameless.[90] "Respectful" comes from the Greek word for "fear" [*phobos*], but in this context it clearly means respect for her husband *out of* her reverence for God. Peter never told the believing wife to leave her unbelieving husband (cf. 1 Cor. 7:13–16); he told her, in essence, to be a good wife to him.

> Christian wives can have an important part in the church's witness [i.e., their testimony of what God said is true—MY WORDS]. That witness may not be easy. Their husbands have resisted the claim of the gospel. They may ridicule the message and insult their wives. So strong may be their hostility that it

---

88   Kistemaker, *NTC*, 118.

89   There is no good argument here in support of a Christian woman who chooses to *marry* an unbeliever in hopes that she might convert him through her good example; rather, the natural implication is that of a wife who has been converted to Christ since her marriage, but her husband has not. Sadly, in many cases where a Christian woman marries an unbeliever, it is the husband who persuades her to recant her faith, not the Christian wife who converts her husband. Rare exceptions to this do not make marrying an unbeliever a wise or justifiable thing to do.

90   Strong, *Dictionary* (electronic), G53.

is no longer possible for their wives to speak of the Lord to them. Even then the Christian wife must not despair. She still possesses a mighty weapon for winning her husband to the faith; it is the testimony of her life. Her husband has refused to heed the word; very well, let him be won *without words*. The silent eloquence of his wife's pure and reverent behavior can preach daily the transforming power of Jesus Christ.[91]

In other words, it is not only through literal preachers that the gospel may be proclaimed. In a more general sense, Peter speaks to what Jesus meant concerning the effect of our "good works" on believers (Mat. 5:16).

A Christian wife's "adornment"—i.e., the way she presents herself to others—must emphasize spiritual purity over "external" beautification (3:3).[92] Peter gives examples: "braiding the hair, and wearing gold jewelry, or putting on dresses." This does *not* mean that such things cannot be done; he is making a contrast, not a condemnation. Braiding (or plaiting) one's long hair—especially with beads, ornaments, and/or ribbons—was often a show of great pride or vanity in the ancient Oriental culture; it was also used as a sign of status (of wealth, prominence, or power). Similarly, the wearing of jewelry or elaborate dresses has long been something that has preoccupied women, even to the neglect of their moral purity (see Isa. 3:16–26 for God's scathing rebuke of this).

But this does not mean that every Christian woman who braids her hear, wears a gold ring, or dons a beautiful dress is violating Scripture. Peter stresses godly attitude, pure intent, and reverence for God (3:4). The "hidden person of the heart"—what Paul calls the "inner man" in Rom. 7:22 and Eph. 3:16—indicates something not visible but is determined

---

91 Clowney, *Message*, 130.

92 "Adornment" here is from *kosmos*, a Greek word that most often is translated in the NT as "world" (as in John 3:16). Literally, it refers to an organized arrangement of something; a decoration or ornamentation; the orderly whole of something. Peter uses it to indicate the way a woman decorates herself; in fact, our modern word "cosmetics" is derived from this same usage (Robertson, *Word Pictures*, on 3:3).

by one's conduct. Christian character is not revealed outwardly (in adornment), but inwardly (in the "fruit of the Spirit"—Gal. 5:22–23).[93] Just as the "outer man is decaying" (2 Cor. 4:16), so the outward adornments are earthly, temporary, and decaying. One's inner person, however, will carry into eternity; her inward nature is "imperishable" in this sense.

The "gentle and quiet spirit" of a woman—not her apparel or cosmetics—is "precious" to God: "that which is highly esteemed among men [and women!—MY WORDS] is detestable in the sight of God" (Luke 16:15).[94] "Quiet" comes from the same Greek word for "quiet" in 1 Tim. 2:12; there, as here, it does not mean "forbidden to speak" but non–disruptive, non–abusive (in speech), and respectful in conduct, especially toward one's husband. "Spirit" here does not mean soul, as it often does in the NT, but (in context) a Christian wife's disposition, the way she carries herself.

The primary subject here (in 3:1–6) is *submission*. The "holy women" in ancient (biblical) times understood this concept and put it into practice regarding their husbands. Peter is not talking about the exceptions— women who rebelled against God and thus their husbands—but those who "hoped in God" (3:5). These women put their trust and confidence in God, and thus believed that He would take care of them if they conducted themselves according to His will. This makes a wife's submission to her husband *not* a marital issue, but a *faith* issue: it is her faith in God—not her husband—that compels her to submit herself in this way.

"Holy women" are those who adorn themselves not only modestly and discreetly (regarding clothing), but with obedience (to God) and

93   "The contrast which Peter develops between *outward* and *hidden*, and between visible to men and seen by God, together with the deeper enduring spiritual values thereby emphasized, is in principle directly parallel to our Lord's teaching in Mat. 6:1–18" (Stibbs, *TNTC*, 125).

94   "Paganism despised the person who was not masterful, who did not assert his own will and make others bow to it; Christianity elevated lowliness and did not regard it as a form of weakness but as a mark of inner, spiritual strength" (Lenski, *Interpretation*, 132).

submission (to their husbands). Peter cites Sarah, the wife of Abraham, and her submissive regard for her husband (Gen. 18:12). The use of "lord," in the most general sense, simply recognizes one who is in charge.[95] By following in her footsteps, Christian women become her "children" (or, "daughters") in the sense that they regard her as their mother who teaches them how to conduct themselves properly toward their husbands (Titus 2:3–5). The fact that Peter instructs women to do this "without...fear" (3:6) indicates this is not always easy. Women might see this as a loss of power or control in the marital relationship; some might think this makes themselves look weak, fragile, or incapable; husbands might take selfish advantage of their wives' submission; etc. Even so, it is the *right* thing to do—and *this* is what finds favor with God (recall 2:18–20, in principle).

The Husband's Responsibility (3:7): Now Peter turns to Christian husbands (3:7). "In the same way" means that the overall topic of submission (in various contexts) has not changed. Just as wives are to subject themselves to God and thus submit to their husbands, so husbands are to subject themselves to God and thus take proper care of their wives. "In an understanding way [or, according to knowledge]" indicates that there is an acceptable and unacceptable "way" to treat one's wife—and God is the One who determines which is which. To "understand" one's wife does *not* mean that a man will fully know, comprehend, and appreciate all it means to be a woman, wife, and/ or mother. This is not only an unrealistic expectation; it is literally impossible since he is a *man* and not a *woman*. (The reverse is also true: women may be more intuitive about men *than* men, but a woman is *not* a man and can never know what it truly means to be one.)

Rather, the Christian husband can and is expected to learn how to live with his wife in a godly and harmonious relationship that honors God and emulates the sacred union between Christ and His church (Eph.

---

95 We should not assume from this passage that all wives must call or even refer to their husbands as "lord." There needs to be a distinction made between *principle* and *application*. Whatever respectful address of one's husband is expected in each culture is acceptable (application), but it must be done for the purpose of biblical submission, not in slavish subjection (principle) (Kistemaker, *NTC*, 123).

5:25–31). The "understanding" required of him, then, is not something beyond his ability but is well within it; even so, he needs to *learn* what is necessary and then *apply* it appropriately. Peter is saying, in so many words, "She is different than you; make every effort to learn and appreciate the difference, and respect the fact that God made her as a *complement* to you—to fulfill what you lack without her. Therefore, do not despise her, belittle her, or hold her in contempt, but honor her as God intended."

The phrase "someone weaker [or, weaker vessel], since she is a woman" (3:7) has led many to believe that women are mentally, emotionally, and even spiritually weaker than men; that they are inferior, feeble, less capable than men; that they are fragile, easily broken, and gullible; and similar demeaning or stereotypical conclusions. Such thoughts have been subjectively imposed upon the text; they are not what Peter is saying. Rather, he is simply admitting the fact that she is different than a man. **First,** she has a different composition than a man; she thinks and sees things differently; she *needs* and *loves* differently; she even *suffers* differently. And, in most cases, she is—through no fault of her own—physically weaker than her husband. **Second,** she is "weaker" with respect to her subordinate role—as the one who submits versus the one to whom submission is given. Just as a slave is weaker in authority than his master (recall 2:18–20), so the wife is weaker in authority than her husband. **Third,** Peter is *not* talking about the moral inferiority of women *or* the moral superiority of men; as Christ sees us, we are all equals, irrespective of gender (Gal. 3:28). Thus, a husband ought not only to regard his wife as one who bears the responsibility of being in subjection to him (and its attending difficulties), he must also regard her as a "fellow heir" of the kingdom of God (Eph. 3:6). This can only be true, of course, if both the husband and his wife are faithful Christians.

How a man treats a fellow Christian may determine whether that man will see "life" in the hereafter (Mat. 25:31–46, Rom. 14:4–10, 1 Cor. 8:11–12, 1 John 4:20–21, etc.). If this is true in a general sense (in the brotherhood), it is especially true in a specific one (in the marriage of two believers). A Christian man who, for example, holds his wife in contempt, treats her with dishonor, deals with her harshly or unfairly, etc., is mistreating someone for whom Christ died. Such disrespect has devastating consequences. Peter warns that a man's prayers will be "hindered [lit., impeded, prevented, or interrupted]" in such cases. Without prayer, he cannot have forgiveness of sins, the ability to petition God, or fellowship with Christ. It is extremely important, then, that a Christian husband treats his Christian wife as she really ought to be regarded—as a servant of Christ.[96] "Our relationships with God can never be right, when our relationships with our fellow–men are wrong."[97]

Living with a Good Conscience
(1 Peter 3:8–22)

The Christian Life Summarized (3:8–12): "To sum up" (or, "Finally"), Peter now addresses *all* Christians—men, women, single, married, divorced, widowed, slaves, and masters—on rendering submission where submission is due, even to one's own hurt (3:8–12). The opposite of submission is insubordination, wherein a person refuses to comply or cooperate with those in authority over him. The authority here is not one's government, master, or spouse; it is God Himself, as expressed through His word. One who resists the teaching of God's word is also insubordinate to God, regardless of any claims of sincerity, faithfulness, or having a "good heart" (as is so popular today).

---

96   "Peter views the believing husband and wife as a kind of church in miniature … a household church, with husband and wife living together as a praying community and 'co-heirs' of salvation" (Michaels, *WBC*, 170–171). Whether Peter *does* view the marriage of two Christians as a miniature church cannot be known for certain, but this does give us another way to consider the sacred union of marriage and (thus) why it is so important that a husband and his wife both treat each other with honor and respect. "When a believing husband and wife do not respect each other as equals [i.e., as "fellow heirs" in the faith; see also Eph. 3:6], their prayers are hollow and their hope uncertain" (*ibid.*, 172; bracketed words are mine).

97   Barclay, *Letters*, 265.

"Harmonious" (3:8) means "like–minded," especially regarding the Christian faith.[98] This is like the "same mind" phrase that Paul uses (Rom. 12:16, 15:5, 1 Cor. 1:10, and Phil. 2:2). "Sympathetic" means to suffer or rejoice with someone, i.e., have compassion or like–feeling for someone (Rom. 12:15). "Brotherly" [Greek, *philadelphos*] means to love one another as brethren or family.[99] "Kindhearted" means having a tender or soft heart toward one another (Eph. 4:32), rather than being quick–tempered, critical, or judgmental.[100] "Humble in spirit" means just what it says: being humble and lowly, and putting others' interests ahead of one's own (Phil. 2:3–4). "Not returning evil for evil ..." (3:9) means not seeking vengeance, retaliation, or self–vindication. Such is Jesus' teaching (Mat. 5:38–42) and Paul's (Rom. 12:17–21). Retaliation for injustices or insults is the opposite of suffering for what is right. Rather than repaying the evil that is inflicted upon us, we are to give "a blessing instead"—we are to pray for our enemies and do good to them.

Peter ends this verse with a reminder that if we wish to be blessed with an inheritance from God, we are to show godly love toward our enemies and not stoop to their level. Since Christians are "called for the very purpose" of being blessed, we should generously give blessings to others.

> All through the New Testament there rings this plea for Christian unity. It is more than a plea; it is an announcement that the Christian cannot live the Christian life, unless in his personal relationships he is at unity with his fellow–men; and that the Church cannot be the Christian Church, if there are divisions within it. ... The more seriously we take the New Testament, the more urgent and painful becomes our sense of the sinfulness of the divisions, and the more earnest our prayers and strivings after the peace and unity of the Church on earth.[101]

---

98 Vincent, *Word Studies* (electronic), on 3:8.

99 *Ibid.*, on 3:8.

100 The KJV has "pitiful" here, which used to mean "tender–hearted," but now has taken on a negative sense, as something that is deficient and therefore warrants obligatory pity or even contempt. Remember that the KJV was written in what is now 400-year-old English, and many of its words are archaic or have changed in meaning.

101 Barclay, *Letters*, 267.

To underscore these brief but potent instructions, Peter cites (in 3:10–12) from the OT (Psalm 34:12–16). The message is basic, clear, and important. Those who strongly desire life, love, and "good days"—those who wish to walk with God—must live accordingly. A person cannot hope to be with God who refuses to conform his heart and behavior to what God expects of His people (recall 1:13–16). This conformity includes refraining from speaking evil of others; not lying ("speaking deceit") but always telling the truth (Eph. 4:25); turning *from* evil and pursuing *good* instead (1 Thess. 5:21–22); and actively promoting peace, "so far as it depends on you" (Rom. 12:18; see Heb. 12:14). God is well–pleased with those who seek righteousness and will listen to their prayers (Isa. 66:2b, Mic. 6:8). But He is "against those who do evil" (3:12)—He is not merely in disagreement with them, but they will face His wrath and judgment (Rom. 1:18). This is especially true in the case of those who injure or persecute His chosen people: He will rise to their defense in the end.

Suffering for What Is Right (3:13–17): Now Peter asks rhetorically, "Who is there to harm you …?" (3:13). The fact is, there are *many* who can "harm" believers, but that is not his point. Rather, there is only so much that people can do to us: first, because they cannot do more than kill the body (Mat. 10:28); second, because God will not allow more than we can bear (1 Cor. 10:13). God is not promising Christians unlimited and guaranteed protection against all harm, nor should we expect this. On the other hand, God *does* promise to put boundaries around how much, how long, how many, and how often such harm will be inflicted—and we are to trust Him in this. As Paul says, "Who will bring a charge against God's elect?" (Rom. 8:33a)—again, *many* can do so, but none of their charges will be sustained, just as all the charges brought against Jesus were nullified by God's vindication of Him. If we do what Jesus did—entrust our souls to the One who judges righteously (recall 2:23)—He will rise to our defense. "If you prove zealous for what is good" means that this providential care is conditioned upon obedient faith. No Christian should expect God to help him if he refuses to pursue "what is good."

When a Christian *does* "what is good," it is very possible that he will receive some kind of backlash or negative response for this (3:14). "For the sake of righteousness" modifies the *kind* of suffering Peter has in mind, which is exactly what Jesus said (Mat. 5:10). Many people suffer for all kinds of reasons; not all suffering is "for the sake of righteousness." One is "blessed" by God only when he is doing what is right, since this finds favor with Him; he seeks a higher objective than his personal comfort or safety; and he trusts that He will take care of him (James 5:11).

"And do not fear …" is a loose paraphrase of Isa. 8:12, but one would do well to read the entire passage (Isa. 8:9–22) to understand its full context and why Peter cited from it. In Isaiah's day, there were many false prophets, spiritists, mediums, and unbelievers in Israel; God told Isaiah not to fear *them* or *their* words, but to fear *Him* and *His* words. So it is today: we are not to fear the loud, intimidating rhetoric of godless people, but are to stand firm in what God says is right and true (Psalm 27:1, 46:1–3). The rhetoric will soon be silenced, one way or another. God's truth is indestructible and eternal; it will never be diminished or silenced.

Instead of being fearful and intimidated, the believer is always to be ready to defend his trust in God to anyone who would question him about it (3:15). He should fear Christ above mere men; this "fear" is meant in both senses (actual fear *and* reverence; see Isa. 8:13). This should only be done if he has *first* sanctified Christ as Lord in *his* heart— that is, if he treats Christ *as* Lord by doing what He says (Luke 6:46, John 14:15) *and* honors His holiness through his own good conduct (recall 1:13–16). To "sanctify" means to set apart, make holy, or make sacred. Christ is holy regardless of anyone's decision otherwise, but the believer makes Christ holy to *himself*—and this sets in motion a life of servitude to Him. To make Christ holy (to oneself) means to regard Him as a divine being; be holy out of respect for Him; and present Him as holy to others, especially in one's defense of His gospel.

"Defense" is from the Greek word *apologia*, from which we get "apology." In ancient times, an "apology" had nothing to do with trying to rectify a wrongdoing but referred to a defense of one's belief or a clearing of one's name (as in Acts 25:16, 1 Cor. 9:3, 2 Tim. 4:16, etc.).[102] The believer is not to literally *apologize* for being a Christian; rather, he is to *defend* the Christian faith. It seems that those who would "ask" for this defense would be those who are interested in having it explained to them, not those who simply wish to mock or denounce it. Peter says, in essence, "Have a ready answer for such people; if Christ *is* your Lord, be ready to prove why you made Him so."[103] A good response might persuade someone else to believe in Him as well.

But even in the case where the believer's faith is ridiculed, "keep a good conscience" (3:16)—i.e., do not do or say anything you might regret, that is uncalled for, or that is simply unchristian. Besides being the right thing to do, the reason for this is to shame the one who mocked or slandered, especially when one's defense of the gospel proves far superior to the mocker's foolish position. Yet, no matter how good one's argument is for what he believes, failing to live accordingly will undermine it. "Bold words will not honor the Lord if they are not supported by a consistent life."[104] "For it is better … that you suffer for what is right rather than … what is wrong" (3:17)—a major theme in Peter's epistle (recall 2:20; see 4:15–16). God is honored when we choose to suffer for His name's sake; He is dishonored when His people's words or behavior descends to that of the ungodly. In fact, God may *want* His people to suffer to bring about something far better than what the absence of suffering would have accomplished.[105]

---

102 Robertson, *Word Pictures* (electronic), on 3:15.

103 "It is said that every citizen in Athens was expected to keep himself sufficiently informed in civic affairs to be able to participate intelligently in any discussion thereof. Christians should be equally well informed in the things of God and as skillful in their presentation" (Woods, *Commentary*, 98).

104 Clowney, *Message*, 151.

105 "When a Christian growls and grumbles or accuses God of injustice for letting him suffer he, of course, spoils it all. He no longer has the glory of suffering innocently. This is gone, he should hang his head in shame" (Lenski, *Interpretation*, 152).

What Christ Accomplished (3:18–22): Suffering for what is right—
and enduring great hostility for doing so—has already been exemplified
in Christ (3:18; see Heb. 12:3).[106] Not only did He suffer dearly, but He
gave up His life to bring much good to God and His people. "Once for
all" indicates the supreme importance of His death: it is unique in all of
history; it does not need to be repeated; it accomplishes what no other
death or sacrifice could accomplish (Heb. 7:27, 10:10–14); it is flawless,
perfect, and unparalleled. "The just for the unjust" means the righteous
(before God) for the unrighteous; or the innocent for the condemned
(Rom. 5:6, 2 Cor. 5:21). "So that He might bring us to God"—indicating
a purposeful, intentional, and planned death (John 12:32, Acts 2:22–23,
etc.).

It took Christ's ordeal on the cross—His innocence, suffering, blood,
and death—to reconcile us to God (Col. 1:19–20). No other death
and no other thing could have done this for us; no one else could have
saved us. He was literally, physically, and historically "put to death in
the flesh"—His was not a figurative or imaginary death. He came to this
world (John 1:14) and died in this world (John 19:32–33) as a real–life,
flesh–and–blood, and identifiable human being. "But made alive in the
spirit"—not kept alive, but (so the Greek) *made* alive, referring to His
resurrection from the dead (Rom. 8:11 and Eph. 2:5).

"In the spirit"—whether in Christ's spirit or the Holy Spirit, since both
can apply here (see Rom. 8:9, for example)—Christ had already *been
active* in proclaiming the truth, even before His incarnation (3:19).[107]

---

106 Some scholars have noted a great similarity between 1 Peter 3:18 and 22, and
1 Tim. 3:16 (Kistemaker, *NTC*, 22–23). Both passages have the same essential
message; both may have been (or become) ancient hymns among the early Christians.
Yet, it could also be that both letters had the same source of authority, namely, the Holy
Spirit, and this would account for any overlapping themes, corroborative theology, and
common expressions of thought, especially if such things were taught *to* the church by
the apostles from the very beginning.

107 It is debatable whether the Greek *pneuma* here should be translated in the lower
case ("spirit") or upper case ("Spirit"), especially given Rom. 8:11. In the original
Greek manuscripts of the NT, *all* letters are capitalized; it is the translators' discretion
as to when a word should be upper or lower case. Given the context, either decision is
acceptable; however, it is my opinion that "Spirit" is more natural to the subject and has

Some think this verse describes His activity *in–between* His death and resurrection, as though Jesus went to preach to certain souls in the spiritual realm to convince them to obey the gospel. This idea undermines the entire premise *of* the gospel—namely, that this life is the only opportunity to prove one's love, loyalty, and obedience to God. This scenario also creates unanswerable and even ridiculous questions: How can these souls *live* by faith when they see all that human faith is *unable* to see? How can they be a "living and holy sacrifice" to God (Rom. 12:1) when they are no longer in the realm *of* the living? How can souls repent of their sins in the hereafter? How can they demonstrate their obedience? What is the *point* of preaching to those who cannot respond to it? Why did Jesus allegedly go only to a limited number of "spirits in prison," and not any—or *all*—other souls?

"Proclamation" here (3:19) is without a specific reference—many assume it is "the gospel," but the text does not say this—and can only be understood by the context *and* corresponding biblical passages. God was "proclaimed" in the ancient world as men called upon Him (Gen. 4:26, 12:8, etc.); Christ, in His pre–incarnate existence ("in the spirit"), was behind that proclamation (recall 1:10–11).[108] Peter does not say, "Christ, after He died, went in the spirit to speak to spirits of men who are now dead." Rather, he says (in paraphrase), "Christ had already *made* a proclamation—namely, through righteous men like Noah [see 3:20–21]—to those men who are *now* dead and whose spirits are *now* in the spiritual realm." If Christ could preach to Gentiles through Paul (Eph. 2:17), certainly He could have preached to people through Noah.

---

better substantiation than "spirit" (see also Clowney, *Message*, 158–9).

108 Commentators often bring up the possibility that Jesus went and preached to *demons* in the spiritual world—since "spirit" is often a reference to demons in Jesus' ministry. (This was apparently first introduced by Friedrich Spitta in the late 19th century; see Kistemaker, *NTC*, 144.) Specifically, these demons/fallen angels are those that allegedly mated with women during Noah's day (a creative interpretation of Gen. 6:1–2, yet contradictory to Mat. 22:30), or possibly their offspring (Michaels, *WBC*, 207–208). But this is all fanciful conjecture. And what would Jesus' visit to fallen angels in the spiritual realm accomplish? These beings are already condemned; did Jesus need to remind them *how* condemned they are? Why did Jesus preach to *those* demons and no others? Clearly, Peter has in mind some reference to *salvation* (especially by involving Noah and his having been "saved" through the water), which is never offered to spirits (fallen angels/demons), but only to *human beings* (Heb. 2:16).

Peter is not offering a second chance to such spirits; instead, he is saying that Christ has been preaching the truth—in essence, giving a ready defense *of* the truth—throughout all of human history, whether through His own mouth or through the mouths of His servants and prophets.[109] As to these departed spirits, they were *once* "disobedient" (in this life) but they are *now* "in prison" (in the afterlife) (3:19b–20a). While on this earth, they made their choice, and they chose to ignore the preaching of God (Gen. 6:5); now they await the final sentencing for their crimes.

Now Peter gives specific biblical and historical context to the point to which he has been leading: "in the days of Noah" (3:20; see Gen. 6:1–18). On what occasion did all this proclaiming occur? Not when such men were dead, but when they were *alive*, specifically, "when the patience of God kept waiting *in the days of Noah*" (emphasis added).[110] Noah was a righteous man who walked with God. His good behavior

---

109 The argument is advanced, in essence, "What is to happen to those who lived before Jesus Christ, and those who never heard His gospel preached?" Unhappy with this scenario, many have thus assumed that the mercy and grace of God must provide all those who died in their sins an opportunity to hear the gospel *in the realm of the dead* and (somehow—inexplicably) repent of their sins, believe in Christ, and (being "born again" without baptism) become *Christians*. (Just as inexplicably, these can deny themselves, take up their crosses, and follow Jesus—and be faithful to Him until death [Mat. 16:24, Rev. 2:10].) This is a "different gospel" than what we read in the NT. But why stop with those who died in their sins? What about all the men and women prior to the time of Christ who died in their *faith*? They also never saw Christ nor heard His gospel preached. How then were they *saved*? They were saved *by* their faith, and the grace of God was imparted to them *because* of their faith, because "the righteous {man} shall live by faith" (Hab. 2:4, Rom. 1:17). So then, no one needed to have seen Christ or hear His gospel in the time before His incarnation; he simply had to live by faith in God—whatever this required of him at the time. Those who lived by faith are saved by grace; those who refused to live by faith are lost, and will forever remain lost, by their own decision. Those who were prevented from *knowing* about God in any way, we will let God decide what to do about them. But we have no right to create a doctrine out of thin air to gratify our emotional *assumption* about what God's mercy and grace ought or ought not to do.

110 The ESV, for example, translates the Greek word here [*hote*] as "because," but then adds a margin note for an alternate reading of "when." *Hote* always has a reference to time ("when"), not conditions or causes ("because") (Strong, *Dictionary*, G3753). Such translations (in the ESV) are undoubtedly an attempt on the part of the translators to sway the text to one conclusion or another, but can be, in my opinion, manipulative.

and words of truth gave opportunity for his generation to obey God, even though no one listened (Heb. 11:7). Likewise, the faithful Christian can show reverence and obedience to Christ—despite the world's mocking, resistance, and condemnation—and thus "proclaim the excellencies of Him who has called [him]" (recall 2:9).

While there were very many people on the earth during the time of the Flood, only eight persons were "brought safely through the water."[111] Water serves as a dual agent of God's divine action: on the one hand, water destroyed all who were not on the ark; on the other hand, those who *were* on the ark were safely brought "through" the water. In this latter case, water provided a means of conveyance from one point to another, but it also served as a transition from one *life* to another.[112] The world that Noah lived in for 600 years was thoroughly destroyed; the world he stepped into upon leaving the ark was, for all intents and purposes, a new world—a new life, new beginning, and fresh start. This scenario is analogous to the conversion process by which one becomes a Christian. While the water of baptism puts the "old self" to death, it also brings to person life a "new creation" formed "in Christ Jesus" (Rom. 6:3–7, Eph. 2:10). "Therefore if anyone is in Christ, he is a new creature; the old things passed away; behold, new things have come" (2 Cor. 5:17). As it was for Noah regarding his physical salvation, so it is for the believer in Christ regarding his spiritual salvation.[113]

---

111 "Eight persons" includes: Noah and his wife, and his sons (Shem, Ham, and Japheth), and their wives (Gen. 6:18). The number eight is significant here, as it is quite often used in Scripture to symbolize a new beginning, new power or strength, new era, or new dynasty. The eighth is also the first (e.g., the eighth day is also the first day of a new week), since it begins a new cycle, era, or dispensation of time.

112 I discussed the importance and symbolism of water as a means of *separation* and *identification* in my book, *Being Born of God: The Role and Significance of Baptism in Becoming a Christian* (Spiritbuilding Publishers, 2014); go to www.spiritbuilding.com/chad.

113 We should not assume that just because God saved Noah and company from *physical* death, therefore He also saved them from *spiritual* death. "By providing the ark, God saved Noah and his family from the judgment of the flood. That deliverance, however, did not in itself give eternal life to the eight persons that were spared. Like the exodus liberation, it was a symbol of God's final salvation from all sin and death" (Clowney, *Message*, 164).

Peter immediately makes this same connection (3:21). "Corresponding" to Noah's being saved through the same water that brought death to other men, so we who are Christians have been "saved" through the water of baptism that simultaneously brought death to our "old self." "Corresponding" is translated from a Greek word [*antitupos*] which is transliterated as "antitype" (used only here and in Heb. 9:24).[114] Noah's scenario provides the type—the shadow, prefigure, or likeness; baptism provides the antitype—the substance, reality, and true form. "Baptism now saves you"—these are Peter's words, not ours. The water of baptism "saves" us similarly to how the water of the Flood "saved" Noah, as a transition from one life (or state of being) to another. While water is used as an *agent* of salvation (e.g., Acts 22:16), the actual *power* of salvation rests upon God's grace, Christ's blood, and the Spirit's sanctification (Eph. 2:8–9, Titus 3:4–7; recall 1:2–3). However, one who refuses the water also forfeits divine grace, since he has refused to consent to God's terms of salvation (see John 3:3–5, Mat. 28:19, Acts 2:37–38, Rom. 6:3–7, Gal. 3:26–27, Col. 2:9–12, etc.).

Baptism is not about a physical, ritual, or ceremonial cleansing (3:21). It is not to cleanse the body, but the human conscience. Baptism is an act of obedience, and all acts of obedience are also acts of faith. In faithful obedience, a person who seeks God's salvation complies with all He says to do.[115] It is impossible for the sinner to have his conscience

114 Robertson, *Word Pictures* (electronic), on 3:21; Strong's reference for *antitupos* is G499. "There is *tupos*, 'type,' which means a *seal*, and there is *antitupos*, 'antitype,' which means the *impression of the seal*. Now clearly between the seal and its impression there is the closest possible correspondence; the seal and its impression correspond to each other. So there are people and events and customs in the Old Testament which are types, and which find their antitypes in the New Testament. The Old Testament event or person is like the seal; the New Testament event or person is like the impression; the two correspond to each other. In a more modern way we might put it that the Old Testament even symbolically represents and foreshadows the New Testament event" (Barclay, *Letters*, 288–9).

115 If baptism is an act of obedience to God for salvation, then it stands to reason—and can be proved biblically—that one's refusal to be baptized translates to an act of disobedience. One cannot hope to receive God's saving grace through disobedience or defiance. While the method of becoming a Christian has been dumbed down, oversimplified, and even trivialized in modern denominationalism (to gain a wider following), water baptism remains a necessary part of the conversion process in the

cleansed by God unless or until he demonstrates obedient faith in God's commandments.[116] A "good conscience" means that a person is cleared of his guilt and therefore able to answer his accuser (Satan or otherwise), "I am made innocent by God's grace." While the agent of cleansing for the *believer* is the water of his baptism, the agent of cleansing for his *conscience* is the blood of Christ (Heb. 9:13–14, 10:19–22). In faith, the sinner is baptized in response to the gospel's commands; in grace, God applies (in essence) His Son's blood to that person's soul and cleanses him from all sin (1 John 1:7).

All this is possible, however, "through the resurrection of Jesus Christ" (3:21b). God has sufficiently demonstrated His power to purify the human soul of sin by having raised His Son from death (recall 1:3; see Acts 17:30–31, Rom. 6:4, 8:11, 10:9–10, etc.). One's baptism, despite his faith and sincerity, would be completely useless otherwise. As it is, Christ's resurrection gives life, meaning, and purpose to one's baptism *into* Him. Not only was He raised from the dead, but Christ has ascended into heaven (Mark 16:19, Luke 24:51, Acts 1:9–11, 2:33, etc.) and is now "at the right hand of God" (3:22). This expression indicates Christ's full authority over all of Creation, second only to His Father who gave Him this authority (Mat. 28:18b, 1 Cor. 15:27–28). Christ's authority extends not only over the visible realm, but over angels and (thus) every spiritual authority as well (Eph. 1:19b–21, Col. 1:15–17).

Peter's reason for providing this information is to encourage those who are suffering in their submission to various people or earthly authorities. If Christ has been exalted to glory after having submitted to these, then certainly the believer will be also (see 5:10).

NT. Again, I highly recommend my book, *Being Born of God: The Role and Significance of Baptism in Becoming a Christian* (Spiritbuilding Publishers, 2014); go to www.spiritbuilding.com/chad.

116   There is a variety of interpretations of "an appeal to God" (NAS): "the answer of a good conscience" (KJV); "the interrogation of a good conscience" (ASV); "the pledge of a good conscience" (HCSB); etc. "Whether Peter is characterizing Christian baptism [his phrase, not mine—CMS] as an 'appeal' or as a 'pledge,' he clearly views it as an act directed from human beings to God, not God's act toward them. ... A purist might properly insist that only God 'saves,' but salvation can be associated either with the divine initiative [grace] or the human response [faith]" (Michaels, *WBC*, 217; bracketed words are mine).

Practical Application of Righteous Living
(1 Peter 4:1–19)

Living for the Will of God (4:1–2): Christ could not have been resurrected *from* the dead (recall 3:22) unless of course He had in fact *died*. His death, then, is what "suffered in the flesh" refers to (4:1). But since believers have been born again (recall 1:3), it necessarily implies that *we also* have died—not literally or "in the flesh," but spiritually and purposefully—and now we live to Christ rather than to sin. Peter—not us—makes the connection between our baptism and our death to sin (recall 3:21). (Incidentally, chapter divisions were not put into this epistle for over a thousand years *after* Peter wrote it; thus, we should read the end of chapter 3 into the beginning of chapter 4 without any separation of thought.) Even so, we must "arm" ourselves to live in allegiance to Christ, and therefore to resist the temptations and sensual lifestyle of this present world. "Arm" here means to "make ready; equip (with weapons)."[117] Peter's battle metaphor also calls to mind Paul's instruction for us to wield the "sword of the Spirit" as we put on the "full armor of God" (Eph. 6:13–18). The idea here is that we are not peacefully walking through life unprovoked by temptations but are constantly under attack and must—with God's help—defend ourselves.

Just as Christ suffered *up to* and *including* His literal death, so we must "with the same purpose [or, mind]" (4:1) be prepared to suffer for what is right (recall 2:21). One who has "suffered in the flesh has ceased from sin"—this refers to believers, not Christ. Christ has never *ceased* from sin since He never *committed* it; He could not have ceased to do what He never began. Obviously, Peter has in mind here the believer who has died to sin in baptism (Rom. 6:3–7 and 2 Tim. 2:11); "in the flesh" indicates the earthly context in which sin wields its power over people. Paul's words are helpful here: "How shall we who died to sin still live in it?" (Rom. 6:2).

---

117 Strong, *Dictionary* (electronic), G3695.

Now, having died to sin, we are to "live the rest of the time [i.e., our lives—MY WORDS] . . . for the will of God" (4:2) rather than for ourselves. The "lusts of men" does not necessarily mean we lived for *other* men's lusts (although, this is possible), but refers here to human lusts (or strong carnal desires) in general—i.e., lusts that are common to the human experience. Giving life to our own lusts creates sin and "brings forth death" (James 1:14–15); living for the will of God brings forth life and peace (James 3:17). "Ceased from sin" does not mean we are *unable* to sin anymore, or that we will successfully never *choose* to sin anymore, but that we will not *practice* sin (1 John 3:4–9).

Not only has the believer already made a choice to serve God, but he has also had plenty of opportunity to serve himself and his carnal desires (4:3). Peter is not by any means giving approval to that former life but is simply recognizing the believer's necessary separation from it. The time of self-gratification is "already past"; such worldly practices must be abandoned altogether, since they are incompatible with one's allegiance to Christ (Rom. 8:6–9, 2 Cor. 6:14 – 7:1, Gal. 5:19–24, etc.). "The desire of the Gentiles" refers to the unconverted heathens in general who have no divine influence to restrain them from sinful indulgences. As a result, they pursued all kinds of behaviors, including:

❏ **"sensuality"**—or lasciviousness, wantonness, or filthy (unrestrained) vice.[118] Our word "sensual" refers to pleasure or gratification derived from fulfilling the human senses (especially, sight and touch), as used in 1 Tim. 5:11 and 2 Peter 2:7.
❏ **"lusts"**—generically, "(strong) desires," but the context often refers to longings for what is forbidden, or sexual immoralities.[119]
❏ **"drunkenness"**—lit., an overflow, surplus, or excess of wine, from a Greek word [*oinophlugiais*] which is only used here in the NT.[120]
❏ **"carousing"**—lit., a letting loose, reveling, riot, etc., often with

---

118 *Ibid.,* G766.

119 *Ibid.,* G1939.

120 Vincent, *Word Studies* (electronic), on 4:3. "It is the *excessive, insatiate* desire for drink, from which comes the use of the word for the *indulgence* of the desire—*debauch*" (*ibid.,* emphases are his). Strong's reference is G3632.

alcohol as the catalyst (only used here and in Rom. 13:13 and Gal. 5:21).[121] The HCSB, NIV, and ESV, for example, translate the Greek word here [*komos*] as "orgies."

❑ **"drinking parties"**—from a Greek word [*potos*] only used here in the NT.[122] It refers to a bout of drinking (wine or liquor), similar to a modern cocktail party with an open bar.

❑ **"abominable idolatries"**—lit., lawless image worship.[123] Of course, *all* image worship is "abominable" to Christians, but particularly any worship that is driven by alcohol, partying, revelry, or self–gratification. The same word for "abominable" [*athemitos*] is used in Acts 10:28, where it is often translated as "unlawful."

With such examples, Peter describes the life that Christians are to have left behind once they died to it and now walk in "newness of life" (Rom. 6:4). However, our friends, family members, co–workers, and others may resent our having left *them* behind in our pursuit of righteous living (4:4). They may be "surprised" [lit., astonished; think it strange][124] that we no longer *desire* to "run" with them and join their worldly behavior. Their question might be: "Since you *used* to do these things with us, and enjoyed it, why would you leave this lifestyle behind? And what do *you* now think about *us*?" Their "excesses of dissipation" [lit., overflowing or flooding of wastefulness or riotous living][125] provide only temporary gratification, always at the expense of their moral, physical, and spiritual well–being (see Rom. 6:21–23).

Even so, not everyone takes kindly to being left behind, and especially when those who leave choose something that the others *know* is better than what they are presently doing. As a result, "they malign you"

---

121 The Greek word [*komos*] implies a village festival. "In the cities such entertainments grew into carouses, in which the party of revelers paraded the streets with torches, singing, dancing, and all kinds of frolics. These revels also entered into religious observances, especially in the worship of Bacchus, Demeter, and…Zeus in Crete" (*ibid.*, on 4:3). Strong's reference is G2970.

122 Robertson, *Word Pictures* (electronic), on 4:3. Strong's reference is G4224.

123 Strong, *Dictionary* (electronic), G111 and G1495.

124 Robertson, *Word Pictures* (electronic), on 4:4. Strong's reference is G3579.

125 Strong, *Dictionary* (electronic), G401 and G810.

(4:4)—"malign" is from the Greek *blasphemeo*, from which we get "blaspheme"—in order to shame, discredit, and even condemn you.[126] The idea is: "If you won't run with *us*, then we will speak evil of *you*."[127] However, such men will "give [an] account to Him" whom they have truly maligned—namely, Christ (4:5; see Jude 1:15). All who speak evil of Christ's people also speak evil of Christ Himself, and we ought to trust that He will vindicate us in the end just as the Father vindicated Him (recall 2:23; see 4:19). His judgment of "the living and the dead" means: He will judge those who are *now* alive as well as those who *have* died, so that no one will *escape* His judgment. Peter does not say when this judgment will occur, but the NT clearly teaches that it will happen; it will happen *after* the physical/earthly system has run its course, and *after* Christ's Second Coming; it will happen in the spiritual realm, not in this life (John 5:28–29, 2 Cor. 5:10, 2 Thess. 1:6–9, Rev. 20:11–15, etc.).

"For the gospel has … been preached … to those who are dead" (4:6)— if "dead" in 4:5 means the physically dead (and we have every reason to believe that it does), there is no reason to believe that suddenly Peter switched to speaking of the *spiritually* dead in the present verse. What Peter means is: the gospel has been preached to men and women who were judged (or maligned; blasphemed) as evil by those who tried to discredit them while they were still alive, but they will be vindicated in the hereafter by the One in whom they believed. They were "judged in the flesh as men"—that is, according to human standards—but "live in the spirit"—that is, while physically dead, they *continue* to live to God, since "He is not the God of the dead but of the living; for all live to Him" (Luke 20:38).

Human judgment is vastly inferior to divine judgment, being biased, short-sighted, and seriously flawed through the lack of knowledge,

---

126 *Ibid.*, G987.

127 JFB (*Commentary* , on 4:4) correctly point out that there is no "you" after "they malign/speak evil," so that the blasphemy these people commit is not really against the *person* (the believer), but against what that person *believes*. We see this in Acts 13:44– 45, for example, when the Jews who resisted the *persons* Paul and Barnabas began blaspheming their *message*. Likewise, when people speak evil of *us* for identifying with Christ, they are in fact blaspheming not us alone, but more specifically that in which (or the One in whom) we believe.

wisdom, and ability. Many will condemn Christians in this life, for all kinds of self-serving reasons, but God will *not* condemn us in the life to come if we remain faithful until our physical death (Rev. 2:10). God's vindication of our faith must, therefore, be infinitely more important to us than whatever people say about us (recall 3:13–14; see Mat. 5:10–12). Those who put their hope in God do not look for the fulfillment of that hope in this life, but in the life to come (Heb. 11:13–16, 39–40).

"The end of all things is near" (4:7a)—but what is meant by "all things"? For Peter to suddenly interject an end-of-the-world comment (as many people assume) makes no sense.[128] It is far more plausible to relate "all things" to the just-mentioned "desire of the Gentiles" (recall 4:3) *and* the Gentiles' maligning of the righteous.[129] Sinful pleasure *and* righteous suffering only last for so long. While it is true that the entire world will be ended (something Peter *does* address in his next epistle), there is no reason to jump to that conclusion here. "All things" means "all the things I've been talking about," not "all things that exist." All those things which godless people practice will soon be coming to an end, which most likely refers to their own deaths, or simply death itself.

"Therefore," Peter warns, "be of sound judgment …" (4:7b). The righteous believer is to exercise sensible, restrained, and appropriate thinking, rather than descend into the alcohol-infused, carnival-like frolicking of worldly people. "Sober spirit" is not only the opposite of literal drunkenness but implies serious-mindedness. While the world

---

128 "Preoccupation with the second coming, particularly by those who have set a date for it, has often led to hysteria rather than sober wisdom. 'Faced by the imminent end of all things the community must not give way to eschatological [i.e., end-of-the-world] frenzy. In such excess it would fall victim precisely to this world' [Ulrich Luck]. Jesus described the faithful servant as 'dressed ready for service' [Luke 12:35–43] and busy as he waited for the returning Lord" (Clowney, *Message*, 178; bracketed words are mine). Woods says that Peter refers to the end of the Jewish system (namely, the destruction of Jerusalem in AD 70) (*Commentary*, 112). While *that* "end" was indeed right around the corner, historically speaking, there is nothing in *1 Peter* to warrant such a conclusion.

129 A general rule in biblical studies, especially when dealing with difficult passages, is that he simplest, most natural answer (given the context) is often the best and most accurate one (with a nod to a principle of critical thinking known as "Ockham's Razor").

drinks, plays, and casts off all inhibitions, the Christian is to be sober, busy with godly work, and focused on what he is doing and where he is going. All this is "for the purpose of prayer," which alludes back to 3:7. If God will not hear the prayers of husbands who refuse to treat their believing wives as "fellow heirs," then He will not hear the prayers of any Christians who are more concerned with having a good time in the world than with seeking first His kingdom and His righteousness (Mat. 6:33).

What We Should Be Doing (4:8–11): Peter now gives basic instructions for all believers that will keep them serious–minded and focused (4:8–11). We should pay special attention to the repeated "one another" phrase since it reveals the close and meaningful relationship fellow Christians are to honor as those "knit together in love" (Col. 2:2).

- ❏ "Above all"—or, in the forefront of these things—"keep fervent in your love…" (4:8a). Love is placed before prayer, because love for God will always lead a person to pray to Him, but prayer without love is useless. (On "fervent" love, see comments on 1:22.) "Love covers a multitude of sins" cannot mean that one's love for another will *hide* a person's sins, or *ignore* them, or automatically *forgive* them. Such teachings are in violation of God's love and His gospel. Rather, it means that Christian love will enable us to see our brother or sister in Christ as a blood–bought child of God, not a hopeless sinner. In doing so, we will not overlook their sins, but will strongly encourage them to *deal rightly* with them (Gal. 6:1–2). Prayers on their behalf, motivated by our love for them, are most appropriate (Luke 22:31–32, James 5:14–16, 20, and 1 John 5:16).
- ❏ "Be hospitable … without complaint" (4:9). "Hospitable" comes from [Greek] *philoxenos*, lit., "loving (or, lover of) strangers."[130] The strangers implied here are not random people on the street, but fellow Christians with whom we are unfamiliar (3 John 1:5–8). We are not to be hesitant, begrudging, or resentful in the kindness (and expense) that we offer to the brethren, since we all belong to God's family *and* will be rewarded with far more than whatever we give up here (Mat. 19:29, in principle).

---

130 Strong, *Dictionary* (electronic), G5382.

- Use whatever "gift" God has given you to His glory *and* the service of the saints (4:10). God has equipped each of us with something to give back to Him in this way (Eph. 2:10). With reference to Jesus' parable (Mat. 25:14–30), we are to follow the example of the five- and two–talent servants, not the one–talent servant, who buried his gift in the ground. "Gift" [Greek, *charisma*] may, in this passage, refer to miraculous gifts the Holy Spirit bestowed upon certain Christians in the early church through the laying on of the apostles' hands (Acts 8:14–17; cf. 1 Cor. 12:4–11). But "gift" does not *have* to be anything miraculous; it can simply refer to whatever special skill, talent, ability, or resource with which God has blessed us to use in His kingdom. (Peter never says anything directly about Christians performing miracles.) In this way, we will be "good stewards"—i.e., effective managers, overseers, or caretakers—of that which God has entrusted to us (see 1 Cor. 4:1–2 and Col. 1:25 [in principle]).
- In the next verse (4:11), Peter is more specific:
  - "Whoever speaks …"—not merely, "Whoever *preaches* God's word," although this *kind* of speaking is included. But all Christians should use their speech (i.e., written words, conversations, social media posts, and all correspondence) in such a way that represents God positively, as He deserves. "Utterances [or, oracles] of God" calls to mind the divine messages of the ancient prophets (as in Isa. 13:1, 15:1, Nah. 1:1, Hab. 1:1, etc.). While our words lack the divine inspiration of those men, we should realize the weight and influence—for better or worse—of our words (Mat. 12:36–37).
  - "whoever serves …"—this can refer to any *kind* of service (as in Rom. 12:4–8). We are to recognize God as the source or supplier of the strength by which we serve. He "[equips] you in every good thing to do His will, working in us that which is pleasing in His sight" (Heb. 13:21); thus, we are not to rest upon our own strength or take credit for our own accomplishments.
  - "so that in all things God may be glorified …"—because God called us *out* of darkness and *into* His light so that we might proclaim His excellencies (recall 2:9). We are not merely to *call* ourselves "Christians" (a mere name); we are to *glorify God through Christ* (an active lifestyle). God deserves to be glorified

(1 Tim. 1:17, Rev. 4:11, etc.), and so does His Son (Rom. 9:5, Rev. 5:12–14, etc.). While unbelievers can offer praises to God, and all the earth proclaims His glory (Psalm 19:1), it is only faithful Christians who are adequately *called* and *prepared* to do so. Thus, "Whatever you do in word or deed, do all in the name of the Lord Jesus, giving thanks through Him to God the Father" (Col. 3:17).

Suffering Is Expected (4:12–19): Now Peter returns to the main subject of his epistle: the need for believers to expect to suffer for what is right (4:12–19). We are not to be "surprised [or, think it strange]" when this happens, since we (ideally) follow the Spirit of God, and the realm of unconverted people follows a very different spirit, producing two incompatible mindsets (4:12; see Gal. 5:16–17).[131] John says virtually the same thing: "Do not be surprised, brethren, if the world hates you" (1 John 3:13), for Jesus promised that it would (John 15:18–25), and indeed it does. A "fiery ordeal" implies not merely a time of difficulty but also purification (recall comments on 1:6–7; see James 1:2–4).[132] The "testing" is not meant to cause believers to *fail*, but quite the opposite— to give them opportunity to *overcome* the trial set before them. It also allows us to "share the sufferings of Christ" (4:13)—just as we share in His death through our baptism, so we share in His suffering for what is right (Phil. 3:10–11). When Christ finally reveals Himself to the world— this can have no other meaning in the NT than His Second Coming—it will be the faithful Christians who "rejoice with exultation" while the ungodly cower in a terrifying expectation of judgment.

Since this is true, to be "reviled [or, insulted; reproached; vilified]" for Christ's name is not a terrible thing, but a *blessed* thing (4:14; see Mat. 5:10–12). "For the name of Christ" modifies or conditions this blessed state. It means that one must first actually *be* in Christ, and then live in

---

131 In 4:4, the ungodly world thinks it strange that Christians will not "run" with them; now Peter warns Christians not to think it strange that ungodly people will be a source of trouble for them. In both cases, there is an element of surprise that remains unfounded and unnecessary.

132 Robertson, *Word Pictures* (electronic), on 4:12.

such a way that *honors* Him. It does not refer, therefore, to someone who merely hijacks the name of Christ for his own purposes or false religion. While the world condemns the person who lives for Christ, God approves of him, and "the Spirit of glory and of God rests upon" him. (This speaks not of two different "Spirits," but the same: He is "of glory" *and* "of God.")

However, this is conditioned upon one's faithful allegiance to Christ, as visibly manifested in his behavior over time. To suffer for Christ is an honor and a privilege; to suffer as a criminal of any sort is dishonorable and common (4:15). Peter provides a sampling of such criminals— murderer, thief, evildoer, and "troublesome meddler."[133] Rather, the only honorable suffering is that which is for the name of Christ—namely, to suffer as "a Christian" (4:16), a true follower of Christ.[134] We glorify God when we accept abuse from others in His name. We are saying, in effect, that His cause is more important than our cause (of saving face, self– protection, seeking vengeance, etc.).

> When the Christian faith permeates society, one of its effects is that the Christian name is a title of respect. … But when Christians are a minority group in society, they frequently are the objects of scorn, reproof, attack, and even persecution. They take the brunt of the devil's fury directed against the followers of Christ. In the early church, the bold confession *I am a Christian* was often heard on the lips of martyrs. In their suffering they

133 The Greek word here is *allotriepiscopos* (G244); "The idea is apparently one who spies out the affairs of other men" (Robertson, *Word Pictures*), on 4:15. While a different Greek word is used in 2 Thess. 3:11 and 1 Tim. 5:13, "busybody" seems to capture what Peter means here.

134 "This word occurs only three times in the N.T. (Acts 11:26; Acts 26:28; 1 Peter 4:16). It is a word of Latin formation coined to distinguish followers of Christ from Jews and Gentiles (Acts 11:26). Each instance bears that idea. It is not the usual term at first like *mathetai* (disciples), saints (*hagioi*), believers (*pisteuontes*), etc. The Jews used *Nazoraioi* (Nazarenes) as a nickname for Christians (Acts 24:5). By A.D. 64 the name Christian was in common use in Rome" (Robertson, *Word Pictures* , on 4:16). On the other hand, there is no reason to think that it was a criminal offense, in Peter's lifetime, to be called (or accused of being) a "Christian." This would, however, become a crime later in the Roman Empire's history.

praised God.[135]

On the *expectation* and *reality* of such suffering, Peter makes it clear:
"it is time for judgment to begin with the household of God" (4:17).
"Judgment" here does not mean punishment, for there would be no
reason for God to punish His "household," nor is a reason here stated.
Rather, it refers to a time of trial, difficulty, or severity that separates
good people from the world, the gold from the ore (recall 1:6–9), or
the men from the boys, so to speak. The idea that this judgment is to
begin with God's household is to reveal its fine virtue, in that it (the
household) will endure successfully and intact because of its divine
protection. The fact that God's people will suffer before the ungodly is
also born out in the book of *Revelation*. God deals with His own people
in a strict manner—i.e., we are not spared trials and testing just because
we *are* His people—for several reasons:

- ❏ to purify the brotherhood of believers. The great tribulation that
  descended upon the early church was not meant to destroy it, but
  to *purify* it and keep it focused upon what was critical rather than be
  distracted with lesser things.
- ❏ to show God's fairness in dealing with *all* men. He will not only
  allow godless people to face the trials of life, but He allows His
  own people to face these *and* the trials of faithfulness as well (Prov.
  11:31). The Christian faces a double burden, not a lesser one,
  compared to that of the unbeliever (2 Tim. 3:12).
- ❏ to show those who contemplate giving their allegiance to Christ
  what such a decision really means, and what it will cost them. This
  is part of what is meant by taking up one's cross to follow the Lord
  (Mat. 16:24, Luke 14:27–33).
- ❏ if God allows His own people to suffer at the hands of the ungodly,
  we can be sure that those who *cause* this suffering will themselves
  be made to suffer (punishment), and that God will vindicate His
  people in due time (2 Thess. 1:6–9; see Rev. 6:9–11).

These reasons answer the unstated question of *why* God will bring
about this judgment in the first place. Peter does not say, "Judgment *may*

---

135 Kistemaker, *NTC*, 179.

come," as though he were suggesting its mere possibility, but that God is *bringing* it (or, *not preventing* this judgment from coming). God always works according to His divine purpose; He never does anything without a specific and excellent reason for doing so, regardless of whether He reveals this to us.

Even though God's people must face severe trials, He still protects them from *too much* and thus continues to protect them (1 Cor. 10:13). The ungodly, however, have no such protection or limitation, and thus will suffer greatly when faced with their own trials. "Those who do not obey ... God," "the godless man," and "the sinner" all refer to the same people (4:17–18); likewise, "Christian," "the household of God," and "the righteous" are all used synonymously. Peter also admits what is true no matter what Christians face or do not face: "it is with difficulty that the righteous {person} is saved."[136]

There is nothing easy about following Christ; if it *seems* easy, we do not yet understand what it requires of us; if it *feels* easy, we are likely not doing it correctly. While salvation is always possible, it is never undemanding; even on relatively good days, discipleship to our Lord will challenge us. Peter asks rhetorically, in so many words, "If salvation can only be obtained *with* God's help, then how in the world (literally!) will anyone be saved *without* it?"

"Therefore"—since all that Peter has said up to this point is true and relevant—we who suffer *for* God should also entrust our souls *to* His divine care (4:19), as did also Jesus (recall 2:21ff) and Paul (2 Tim. 3:11–12). There is no one who *can* protect our souls but He who is more powerful than all men, all forces of nature, and even all "spiritual forces

---

136 Some versions here translate the Greek word as "scarcely," which may seem to convey the idea that we will only be saved *just barely*, as if *by the skin of our teeth*. This does not speak well of God's power, but makes it sound like *He* can barely save us, which undermines the *power* of salvation itself (Rom. 1:16, 1 Cor. 1:18). Even if "scarcely" is used here, it means "with difficulty" (see Acts 14:18, 27:7–8, 16, and Rom. 5:7)—not with *God's* difficulty, but with the difficulty of us maintaining our faith amid various trials. "[Peter] does not imply uncertainty of the outcome, but the difficulty of the road that leads to it" (Samuel Benetreau, quoted in Clowney, *Message*, 195; so Michaels, *WBC*, 272).

of wickedness" (Eph. 6:12). God, our Creator, certainly has put into motion a plan for humankind, and especially for His people. He will not abandon us (Heb. 13:5b–6); He will never leave us to suffer without hope or a way of escape from being overwhelmed by this world. "For God has not destined us [i.e., His church—MY WORDS] for wrath, but for obtaining salvation through our Lord Jesus Christ, who died for us" (1 Thess. 5:9–10a).

God is not only our Creator, and thus knows us well and knows what we need the most, but He is "faithful" to provide for us.[137] This refers to His trustworthiness, dependability, and reliability; He does not waver in His ability to save us or His concern for us; He is not one day "all in" but indifferent or indecisive the next. He is, therefore, *worthy of our trust*—even when we must face difficulties that we do not understand. Our inability to explain God's plan does not make Him any less "God," does not make Him unfaithful to His plan, and does not imply that there is *no* plan. God is always faithful to us—He is never the variable in our relationship with Him—but whether *we* remain faithful to Him is yet to be seen.

Final Exhortations
(1 Peter 5:1–10)

So far in his epistle, Peter has spoken to Christians who are undergoing persecution; citizens under a secular government; servants to earthly masters; wives; husbands; tempted to follow their worldly friends; etc. Now he turns his attention directly to church elders (5:1–4). "Elders" in this context does not mean merely "older men," even though that is what the Greek word for "elders" [*presbuteros*] describes.[138] The fact that they are "shepherds" and are to "exercise oversight" indicates a specific role within the church, not merely an age group. Paul defines what these men are to look like (1 Tim. 3:1–7, Titus 1:5–9); Peter talks about their work.

137 Repeatedly, the NT writers remind us that "God is faithful"; see 1 Cor. 1:9, 10:13, 2 Cor. 1:18, 2 Thess. 3:3, Heb. 10:23, and 1 John 1:9.

138 Strong, *Dictionary* (electronic), G4245.

Peter's Instructions to Elders (5:1–4): Peter exhorts church elders as a "fellow elder" (5:1): he is an "elder" to the entire church, whereas these men are elders only in the congregations that appointed them. It is interesting that he does not invoke his apostolic authority here but offers a kind and compassionate encouragement based upon shared responsibilities. But Peter's credentials for offering this exhortation go further: he also has personally witnessed Christ's suffering—His arrest, trials, scourging, and crucifixion—and therefore can speak to the kind of commitment that is necessary for such Christian men to do their job. Moreover, he is "a partaker also of the glory that is to be revealed"— likely, referring to the surety of his salvation, and thus speaking as one who has a shared objective with his fellow elders. "Anyone, who is himself an heir of salvation, may appropriately exhort his fellow– Christians to fidelity in the service of their common Lord."[139]

Now Peter provides specific instructions to these elders. **First,** "shepherd the flock of God among you" (5:2)—because shepherding defines the essential function of the elders' work.[140] Like an actual shepherd, they also have a "flock" (their own congregation—those who are "among you") and are entrusted with the responsibility to tend to its spiritual welfare. This means: "Tend as a shepherd, by discipline and doctrine. Lead, feed, heed: by prayer, exhortation, government, and example."[141] Many elders today see themselves as mere decision–makers for their churches, nothing more; they sit in offices, chair meetings, and carry out administrative duties, but are not directly and intimately connected with their flock. In essence, they adopt a kind of CEO approach to their role, but this misses Peter's point entirely.

---

139 Barnes, *Barnes' Notes* (electronic), on 5:1.

140 "Shepherd" here is from *poimaino*—the verb form of the noun *poimen* ("pastor") in Eph. 4:11—and can be thus translated "pastor" (as a verb), "tend," or even "feed," because feeding is an essential part of tending. Jesus used the same word with Peter when He told him to "Shepherd My sheep" (John 21:16). "Flock" is from *poimnion*, which refers to the group that is to be shepherded (adapted from Robertson, *Word Pictures*, on 5:2).

141 JFB, *Commentary* (electronic), on 5:2.

The proof that the CEO model doesn't work is in the absence of a following, for this kind of leader has no flock. No one comes to such leaders for shepherding, and the troubled and timid know to avoid them. Their voices are not heard because no one is listening. As Jesus said, sheep "will never follow a stranger; in fact, they will run away from him because they do not recognize a stranger's voice" [paraphrased from John 10:5].[142]

In sharp contrast to this picture:

Elders are not strangers merely plugged into a job. Rather, elders are people who already have a flock, who already are serving as shepherds. The process of appointing elders is simply the process of acknowledging those who have been shepherding for a long time. It is recognizing those who have attracted flocks though the genuineness of their lives, the consistency of their service, and the authenticity of their relationships.[143]

Jesus enjoyed a *warm and loving personal relationship* with his trainees. His role was not one of boss to employees. He was not the CEO, with the Twelve somewhere down his payroll "food chain." Jesus did not reside in the officers' quarters while the Twelve bunkered in the barracks. On the contrary, Jesus called them his "friends." He traveled with them, ate with them, even washed their feet. … He connected so authentically that one disciple (maybe all of them) felt that he was the "disciple whom Jesus loved."[144]

Second, elders are to be "exercising oversight" of the flock (5:2). "Exercising oversight" comes from a single Greek word [*episkopeo*]; its use here basically means, "serve in the capacity of an overseer (to your congregation)."[145] The office of an overseer [lit., bishopric, as in

142 Dr. Lynn Anderson, *They Smell Like Sheep*, vol. 1 (New York: Howard Books, 1997), 36; bracketed words are mine.

143 *Ibid.*, 126.

144 *Ibid.*, 104.

145 Strong, *Dictionary* (electronic), G1983.

1 Tim. 3:1] is the *only* office that remains within the NT pattern for church organization since the apostolic office has ended. (Deacons are appointed servants; preachers are ministers of the word of God; neither are officers.[146])

Third, elders are not to exercise oversight "under compulsion [or, not under constraint]" (5:2). A man ought not to enter the eldership only out of dutiful obligation, feeling pressured or compelled to shepherd only because everyone wants him to; no one else will do so; he feels guilty for *not* doing so; or a congregation wants a plurality of elders to avoid having business meetings (!). While being a shepherd of a church of God is a high honor, no one should be *forced* to do so. Rather, Peter says this work ought to be engaged "voluntarily [or, willingly]." Paul says a man ought to "aspire" to this work and "desire" it (1 Tim. 3:1); in both passages, there is no sense of one being mandated to do so, even if his congregation thinks him adequately qualified for the role. Barnes says rightly: "Go cheerfully to your duty as a work which you love, and act like a freeman in it, and not as a slave."[147]

Fourth, elders are to shepherd "according to {the will of} God" (5:2). (The phrase "the will of" has been inserted by translators, being naturally implied.) This regards their work as shepherds; their moral responsibility as overseers; their willingness in volunteering for this work; and, by implication (and what is about to be said), their attitude toward God *and* His people. A further reference might be added (from Titus 1:9): they need to be able to teach the word of God proficiently *and* refute any contradiction to this. A man cannot teach what he does not know, and he cannot refute what is false if he does not know what is true. It is "the will of God" that an elder conduct himself properly in all these considerations.

---

146 For much more detailed information on elders *and* deacons, I recommend my published workbooks on *1 Timothy* and *Titus—1 & 2 Timothy Commentary* and *Titus and James Commentary*, respectively. I also recommend my book, *The New Testament Pattern* (Spiritbuilding Publishers, 2023), which details the roles of elders and deacons in Christ's churches; go to www.spiritbuilding.com/chad.

147 Barnes, *Barnes' Notes* (electronic), on 5:2.

Fifth, elders are never to *be* elders only for financial benefits (compensation or remuneration) (5:2). "Sordid gain" (KJV says "filthy lucre"—an antiquated expression, to be sure) means any kind of monetary profit that is obtained dishonorably or illicitly. Elders are to be "free from the love of money" (1 Tim. 3:3)—this does not mean they cannot *receive* money (because they can—1 Tim. 5:17–18), but that money must never be the reason or incentive for them serving as shepherds and overseers. It is disgraceful for an elder to hijack God's system of governing His church only to receive a paycheck; likewise, it is disgraceful for a man to *remain* an elder—especially when he is not fulfilling its responsibilities—only because he does not want his pay to end.[148] Rather, he is to pursue and fulfill his ministry to God "with eagerness." The Greek word here [*prothumos*] not only means willingly, but also with personal zeal, readiness, and a "forward spirit."[149]

Sixth, elders are never to "lord" themselves over their flock (5:3). This means they are supposed to lead, shepherd, govern, and feed their flock, not flaunt their power or position over it in the role of a king, tyrant, master, or unquestionable ruler. Some elders act like old–time lawmen: they flash their badge, brandish their gun, and boast, "I'm the law around here!" This is contradictory to what Peter instructs. Jesus said that Gentile rulers "lord it over" their subordinates and "exercise authority" over them, but that it is not to be this way with those who serve Christ (Mat. 20:25–26). "Any man who enters an office with the desire for the pre–eminence, with the idea of exercising authority, with the idea of becoming a ruler, has got his whole point of view upside down."[150] Shepherds are to exercise truth, love, and compassion, not self–willed authority.[151]

---

148 "Thus an elder (or, for that matter, any spiritual leader) who obtains money as the result of misuse of his position is as base and disreputable as the extortioner, the trafficker in the bodies of women, and the seller of slaves. Then, as now, some turned religion into a trade and commercialized the gospel of Christ, 'supposing that godliness is a way of gain' (1 Tim. 6:5)" (Woods, *Commentary*, 125).

149 Vincent, *Word Studies* (electronic), on 5:2; Strong's reference is G4290.

150 Barclay, *Letters*, 316.

151 "Whenever a man in the church of Christ claims authority or exercises power merely on official grounds [i.e., citing himself as an "officer of the church"—MY

The only binding authority the eldership can exercise is what has already been decreed in the Scriptures; it does not have any authority of its own. The elders' "charge" (or, realm of responsibility) refers to souls entrusted to their spiritual oversight (Heb. 13:17). One of their primary responsibilities is to serve as an example to these souls (Phil. 3:17, 2 Thess. 3:9, and 1 Tim. 4:12, in principle). Elders who do so are extremely helpful; those who do not will be a detriment to their congregation.

Thus, church elders are to be shepherds for the right reason, with the right heart, and in the right manner. In time, "the Chief Shepherd" will appear—an unmistakable NT reference to the Second Coming of Christ—and those who have been entrusted with various responsibilities will then be called to give account for them (5:4; recall 1:7 and 2:25). The "you" here refers, in context, only to elders who have served well; no reward ("crown") will be given to those who have not. This "crown [or, wreath] of glory" is also known as "the crown of righteousness" (2 Tim. 4:8) or "the crown of life" (James 1:12, Rev. 2:10).[152] It is rewarded by Christ Himself to those who have faithfully and successfully carried out those charges He has given to them. In referencing the *Chief* Shepherd as the one to whom all *other* shepherds answer, Peter is also implying that these shepherds have no right to do anything in their work that would contradict Christ's character or teaching.[153] Even so, his words here are meant far more as a promise

---

WORDS], he is as essentially a pope and claims the prerogatives of papacy as fully as does he of Rome. He may be a smaller one, his sphere of action may be more limited, but the principle is the same. All the evils of the papacy arise out of the claim of the Pope and his council to decide questions by virtue of official position" (David Lipscomb, "Church Authority," quoted in *Restoration Ideas on Church Organization,* J. Ridley Stoop, ed. [Nashville: David Lipscomb College, no date], 82–83).

152 "The Greek word for 'fade away' relates to the amaranth flower, which does not lose its beauty and therefore symbolizes immortality. Skillful hands formed a crown of these flowers; the crown then was given to the victor as a token of his glory" (Kistemaker, *NTC,* 194). "Crown" here is from *stephanos,* a crown of heroes or conquerors, and not *diadema,* the crown of royalty or sovereignty (Woods, *Commentary,* 127).

153 "No member has the right to obey an elder when in so doing he has to go contrary to the word of God in the matter; while, on the other hand, if the elders teach the

rather than a warning.

Peter's Instructions to "Younger Men" (5:5): "You younger men" is contrasted with "elders" (5:5), with reference to age or season of life. In the Greek, however, "younger" refers not exclusively to "men" (it is a gender–neutral term, like "teenagers"), but to those who are younger in age, whether male or female. Likewise, "elders" no longer has reference—since the context has changed—exclusively to male church elders, but to *all* who are older, whether male or female.[154] (Even so, the implication is: just as church elders are not to lord their position over the flock, so those in the flock are not to resist the guidance of their church elders.) Younger Christians are to submit to older Christians; age deserves acknowledgement, respect, and submission (Lev. 19:32, 1 Tim. 5:1–2, and Titus 2:2–5). Not only this, but "all of you"—younger, older, the "flock," and church elders—are to put on humility toward one another (recall 3:8; see Eph. 5:21).

To "clothe" oneself with something means, figuratively, to take on the identity of (as in Rom. 13:14 and Gal. 3:27), or to accept the disposition of (as a mindset or attitude).[155] In essence, Peter says, "Don't just *talk* about being humble, but *look the part*, as if 'humility' were an outer

---

word of God faithfully, and practice it themselves, those that refuse to submit simply refuse the word of God, and thus rebel against God rather than against men. God must be obeyed at all hazards, and Christ must forever remain as Head of the church ..." (E. G. Sewell, "The Fifth Chapter of First Peter—Elders, etc.," quoted in *Restoration Ideas*, 174). "To speak of the Chief Shepherd is to remind the elders that they are only undershepherds. Their authority is not original: they minister only in Christ's name, and according to his word" (Clowney, *Message*, 206).

154 JFB think that "younger men" here refers to deacons submitting to church elders (*Commentary*, on 5:5). However, there is nothing to support this; one must force this idea into the text, as it does not come naturally. The NAS translators, for example, add the word "your" to the text ("be subject to {your} elders"), giving the impression, unnecessarily, that Peter refers to church elders rather than simply older men and women. "Here the antithesis between younger and elder shows that the word refers to age, not to office as in 1 Peter 5:1" (Robertson, *Word Pictures*, on 5:5).

155 "It is quite probable that Peter here is thinking of what Jesus did (John 13:4ff.) when he girded himself with a towel and taught the disciples, Peter in particular (John 13:9ff.), the lesson of humility (John 13:15). Peter had at last learned the lesson (John 21:15–19)" (*ibid.*, on 5:5).

garment that people can see on you." Clothing *originally* was the result of human pride that led to sin (think of Adam and Eve's account, and their realization of their nakedness after having sinned). In contrast to human pride, Christians are to clothe themselves with godly humility which will lead to the "fine linen" of Christ's bride (Rev. 19:7–8). The proud heart—regardless of how it manifests itself—is opposed to God, and therefore God is opposed to it. But God gives divine help ("grace") to the humble (Isa. 66:2b). "Grace" here is not simply God's general kindness that He gives to *all* people, but His *saving* grace that is only given to those who have demonstrated obedient faith in Christ (Eph. 2:8–9).

The Need for Humility (5:6–10): "Therefore"—since God *does* favor the humble—"humble yourselves…that He may exalt you" (5:6). In other words, do not exalt yourself above others; do not assume a status or position that does not belong to you; and—most importantly—do not question God's authority or ability to perform simply because things are not going according to your expectations. To put oneself "under the mighty hand of God" means to surrender to His will and submit to His authority. Those who suppress themselves, God will help; those who attempt to suppress *Him* (or His *righteousness*), He will destroy (Rom. 1:18–20). God will exalt the humble soul "at the proper time"—i.e., at a time of His choosing; in the most proper time; and *for certain* (Isa. 57:15). God will not leave His servants to suffer for the sake of righteousness without finally acknowledging, vindicating, and rewarding them for doing so.

Considering what has just been said, Peter confidently tells his readers to "[cast] all your anxiety upon Him, because He cares for you" (5:7; see Mat. 6:25–34). "Anxiety" here is understood to mean concern, worry, or cares; it refers to whatever distracts us (negatively) from what we should be paying attention to.[156] We are to give these things over to God—in essence, lay them at His feet—because: He is able to handle them; we are *not* able to handle them; He has asked us to do so (Phil. 4:6); He cares for us and does not want us to be overwhelmed.

---

156 Strong, *Dictionary* (electronic), G3308.

To underscore the danger of *not* casting our cares upon God and thus *being* overwhelmed with them, Peter gives several brief but potent directives (5:8–9): "be of sober spirit"; "be on the alert"; "resist [the devil]"; "[stay] firm in your faith."[157] (On "sober in spirit," recall comments on 1:13.) "Be on the alert" means what it says: pay attention; stay vigilant; do not be distracted from your primary responsibility (see Mark 13:35–37, Acts 20:31, 1 Cor. 16:13, and Eph. 6:18). Since the devil [Greek, *diabolos*], a.k.a. Satan, seeks to devour God's people, we must take guarding against his attacks very seriously. He is a powerful adversary (or, opponent); we are unable to resist or contend with him *without divine help*.[158] "Prowling about" indicates stalking after unwary prey (imagine a child abductor, for example, looking for an easy and unsuspecting target).[159] A "roaring lion" carries another aspect of him, namely, his fearsome, intimidating, and brutal assault against God's people. Regarding the individual believer, Satan stalks him stealthily; regarding the brotherhood, he roars with arrogance and contempt—no doubt a reference to the persecution he instigates against the church.[160]

---

157 Peter's brief warnings are in the imperative in the Greek—lit., "Pay attention! Wake up!" (Michaels, *WBC*, 297).

158 As I have said in my other works, it is very important to realize that Jesus and His apostles regarded Satan [Greek, *diabolos*, "the devil"] as a very real, powerful, and insidious enemy. He is not a myth, fairytale, or fictional boogieman; he is a cunning, resourceful, and seductive spirit that has the ability—though we do not fully understand it—to assault people on a spiritual level. On the other hand, he is *not* a divine being, he *can* be curtailed by God's intervention, and he *will* flee from God's divine presence (James 4:7). Powerful as he is, Satan is no match for Jesus Christ (Luke 10:17–20). I discuss Satan and his strategy at some length in my book, *This World Is Not Your Home* (Spiritbuilding Publishers, 2022); go to www.spiritbuilding.com/chad.

159 We are made to think of Satan's "roaming about on the earth and walking around on it" (Job 1:7 and 2:2). On the other hand, we should be careful not to determine NT doctrine about Satan or his doings based entirely upon that account. In *Job*, Satan is not really given a personal name or identity; he is literally "the adversary" (this is how it appears in the Hebrew text); in Peter's account, "the devil" is most certainly an actual character with a distinct personality. Even so, the idea is clear: we are contending with "spiritual forces of wickedness" that are invisible yet very powerful, and therefore we would do well to seek God's protection against them (Eph. 6:10–17).

160 "Naturalists have observed that a lion roars when he is roused with hunger, for then he is most fierce, and most eagerly seeks his prey" (Barnes, *Barnes' Notes*, on 5:8); see Judg. 14:5, Ps. 22:13, Jer. 2:15, etc. God also is depicted as a roaring lion (see Hos.

The word "devour" [Greek, *katapino*] means to drink down, be overwhelmed, or be swallowed up.[161] The devil is not seeking to give us a black eye or a broken arm, but to destroy us.

"But," Peter strongly urges us, "resist him [the devil]" (5:9a)—not by our own strength, authority, or resourcefulness, but with God's. Satan is a force to be reckoned with—but he can be resisted (James 4:7). Jesus resisted him by appealing to God's word (Mat. 4:1–11); we can do the same. But quoting Scripture to Satan *by itself* will not help us. Jesus quoted Scripture *as* He relied upon God's divine protection; we can and should do the same. To resist the devil, we must not dabble in satanic thinking or behavior, or surround ourselves with satanic people (1 Cor. 15:33). We cannot think that the devil will flee from us if we befriend his world (James 4:4). On the other hand, we often underestimate the great providential help that God promises us by turning to Him for our deliverance from Satan (1 John 5:18). "Firm in your faith" means standing strong "in the Lord" (Eph. 6:10–14), and not trusting in our own strength *or* someone else's. Many Christians have made the mistake of trusting in their *religion* (i.e., biblical knowledge, doctrine, traditions, preachers, elders, etc.) rather than *the Lord.* Left uncorrected, this is a fatal error.

Just as the devil went after Job and many other faithful men and women in ancient times, so he will come after Christians (5:9b)—we should not be surprised by this (recall 4:12). There is comfort in knowing that our struggle against the devil is not unique in history, or that we are not being singled out from the rest of the brotherhood. In fact, many Christians throughout the world since the first century have endured far more suffering for righteousness than most of us will ever know. Regardless, "No temptation has overtaken you but such as is common to man," and God is faithful to provide us with a "way of escape" from all of Satan's assaults (1 Cor. 10:13).

11:10) when He takes on the role of an adversary against His own people for refusing to listen to and obey Him. While Satan's power can be stopped, God's power cannot.

161 Strong, *Dictionary* (electronic), G2666. "The suggestion is that of drinking the victim's blood" (Lenski, *Interpretation*, 226); consider Rev. 17:6, for example, considering this.

The phrase "brethren [lit., brotherhood] who are in the world" indicates a limited context in which all such striving against the devil takes place: it is *here*, in this world; it will not happen in the world to come. While suffering for what is right is certainly a trying ordeal when we are directly facing it, such ordeals are limited in time (5:10). "A little while" *here* is set against the eternal glory that we can look forward to in the *hereafter* (see Rom. 8:18 and 2 Cor. 4:17). "So there remains a Sabbath rest for the people of God" (Heb. 4:9), and one of the things we will "rest" from is the devil's ravaging assault against our faith, our conscience, and our soul. Through the grace of God—i.e., by Him doing everything for our salvation that we cannot do ourselves—His calling will reach its full purpose in an "eternal glory in Christ." The following verbs ("perfect," "confirm," "strengthen," and "establish") are actions that God brings about through the suffering process (James 1:2–4 echoes this same thought). "Perfect" (as a verb) means to prepare for success, fully equip, or make complete (Col. 1:28, Heb. 13:20–21). "Confirm" means to establish, determine, or provide support; "strengthen" means what it says—to give strength (Eph. 3:16). "Establish" means to provide grounding, foundation, or stability for something.[162]

Closing Remarks
(1 Peter 5:11–14)

Peter brings his letter to a close with a very brief but fitting doxology (or, hymn of praise): "To Him"—the God of all grace—"be dominion forever and ever. Amen" (5:11). "Dominion" in English has to do with "domain," referring to a region, realm, or jurisdiction over which one rules. Yet, the Greek here [*kratos*] has to do with strength, might, and power (recall 4:11; see also 1 Tim. 6:16).[163] ("Democracy," for example, is from *demos* [people] and *kratos* [power]—lit., the "power of the

---

162 The definitions of these four words are partly based upon Vincent, *Word Studies* (electronic), on 5:10.

163 Strong, *Dictionary* (electronic), G2904.

people."[164]) God deserves reverent acknowledgment as the source of all power. The Christian will not be able to endure this life successfully without his reliance upon God's power and strength; therefore, the source of that strength deserves full recognition and praise. "Amen" means "so be it"; "let it be so"; or simply "*yes*" (2 Cor. 1:18–20).

Using a secretary [lit., *amanuensis*] to do the actual writing of a letter was common in the ancient world, partly because such people were well-trained in writing, grammar, and syntax. Paul often—if not always—dictated his letters; in at least one occasion in the NT, the *amanuensis* added his own written greeting (Rom. 16:22).[165] In the case of the present epistle, it is very likely that Peter writes these closing comments in his own hand (5:12–14), but that he dictated the rest of it to Silvanus (the Latin form of Silas). We assume Silvanus is the same "Silas" that accompanied Paul on what is known as his second missionary journey (Acts 15:40ff); he is described as a "prophet" who was first introduced to us in the Jerusalem council (Acts 15:32). He appears as a co-supporter of Paul's letters (1 Thess. 1:1, 2 Thess. 1:1), and seems to be a mentor for Timothy in that young man's early ministry (Acts 17:14–15, 18:5). He was a Roman citizen, a colleague of Paul, and very likely a man of education and culture. His involvement in this epistle removes the otherwise difficult idea that a Galilean fisherman wrote in what many scholars regard as excellent Greek.[166] Peter regards Silvanus as "a faithful brother"—an understatement, considering the man's involvement in early church history—and he remains one of the unsung heroes of the NT.

The purpose for Peter's having written his epistle is to exhort (or give encouragement to) Christians facing various trials of faith and to give his own authoritative testimony to "the true grace of God" (5:12b).

---

164 *Merriam–Webster's 11ᵗʰ Collegiate Dictionary*, electronic edition (© 2003 by Merriam–Webster, Inc., v. 3.0).

165 Charles W. Draper, "Letters," *Holman's Illustrated Bible Dictionary*, electronic edition, Trent C. Butler, gen. ed. (© 2003 by Holman Bible Publishers; database © 2014 by WORDsearch Corp.).

166 Barclay addresses this situation in his introduction to *1 Peter* (*Letters*, 169–71).

Part of the solemn responsibility of an apostle was to serve as a living eyewitness of Christ and His ministry, resurrection, and ascension (Luke 24:45–48, Acts 1:8, 21–22, 2:32, 5:32, etc.). The "true grace" contrasts with any false teachings or false representations of God's gospel. While Peter does not deal with any false teachers in this epistle, Paul certainly did in his own letters; in other words, the maligning of the gospel of grace was a real and persistent problem (see 2 Peter 2:1–3). "Stand firm in it!" is imperative—not a suggestion, recommendation, or good advice, but a commandment (cf. 1 Cor. 16:13, Eph. 6:11, Phil. 4:1, etc.).

"She who is in Babylon" (5:13) is one of the most mysterious phrases in this epistle. The questions are: First, who is the "she"—is this a person (literal), a specific congregation (figurative), or something unknown to us but known to Peter's primary audience (enigmatic)? Second, is "Babylon" the actual city in ancient eastern Mesopotamia (literal), a specific congregation (figurative), or something purposely vague to us but known by Peter's primary audience (enigmatic)?[167] Commentators and biblical scholars are divided on the final interpretation, though the conservative view strongly leans toward "she" as referring to a church rather than an individual person. This latter conclusion is also supported by the "chosen together with you" phrase. This would be an awkward thing to say of an individual—not to mention that all "chosen/called/elect" references in the NT have to do with *groups* of people—but would be a natural statement regarding a congregation of believers who share the same faith as those whom Peter is addressing (recall 1:1–2).

Supporters of "Babylon" referring to the actual geographical city (in the East) all rely upon supposition rather than anything concrete.[168] There

---

167 Some translators add, "{The church that} is in Babylon…," but "The church that" phrase is not in the Greek text. This is an occasion in which translators cross the line from merely *translating* a language to *teaching* something from their own point of view. It should be mentioned, too, that some believe that Peter is referring to his wife, but this is quite a stretch with zero corroboration (JFB, *Commentary*, on 5:13). We know Peter was married (1 Cor. 9:5), yet he makes no specific reference to his wife in the NT.

168 For example, it is argued that there were many Jews in the "Asiatic dispersion" in literal Babylonia; there were more Jews in literal Babylon than in Rome, the symbolic reference to Babylon elsewhere in the NT (Rev. 18:2, 10, and 21); Peter would not use

is no good evidence that there was an actual church in Babylon, or that Peter ever went there.[169] Not only this, but the actual city of Babylon had been reduced to ruins, per God's prophecies against it, and was virtually abandoned at the time of Peter's writing. (There was also a Babylon in Egypt, but it was nothing more than a small military garrison in Peter's day.[170]) The most natural, fitting, and likely use of "Babylon" was in reference to Rome. This was not a secret code word as much as a symbolic description of that city, as picked up by John in *Revelation*. Just as ancient Babylon served as a captor and oppressor of God's people in exile, so Rome ("Babylon") became to Christians in their figurative exile on this earth (1 Peter 1:1, 2:11, and Heb. 11:13–16). Also, just as Babylon was judged and destroyed by God, so Rome was judged and destroyed. In both cases, such action was predicted prophetically and then carried out historically.[171]

"Mark" (5:13) is, most likely, the same Mark—a.k.a. John (Acts 12:12, 25), and a cousin of Barnabas (Col. 4:10)—that accompanied Paul and Barnabas on the first leg of their so–called first missionary journey (see Acts 13:1–13). (Some, however, have disputed whether this "Mark" is the same Mark mentioned in *Acts*, since Mark was an extremely

---

"Babylon" to refer to Rome in a friendly salutation when the name would describe a "harlot" in later writings (Rev. 17:5); etc. (JFB, *Commentary* , on 5:13). These are not proofs, however, but simply circumstantial statistics or outright opinions. It should be noted, too, that the speculation about "Babylon" referring to anywhere *but* Rome did not arise until the 16th century Reformation (Stibbs, *TNTC*, 176).

169 Lenski, in speaking for many, is adamantly convinced that "Babylon" refers to Rome, and that speculations about Peter being in actual Babylon are completely without support (*Interpretation*, 10–11, 231–232).

170 Clowney, *Message*, 223–224; A. W. Fortune, "Babylon in the NT," *The International Standard Bible Encyclopedia*, electronic edition (© 1979 by Wm. B. Eerdmans Publishing Co.; database © 2013 by WORDsearch Corp.).

171 "At the same time, it is doubtful that all the sinister associations of 'Babylon the Great, Mother of Prostitutes and of the Abominations of the Earth' (Rev. 17:5) are present already in 1 Peter. Peter's earlier admonitions to defer to the Roman emperor and his appointed representatives (2:13–17) preclude a deep–seated critique of the empire or imperial authority. The only thing wrong with 'Babylon' is that it is not home. 'Babylon' at the end of the epistle is simply the counterpart to 'diaspora' at the beginning" (Michaels, *WBC*, 311).

common name in the ancient world.[172]) Mark was also the cause of the strong disagreement between Paul and Barnabas after the Jerusalem council, which resulted in Barnabas taking Mark with him to Cyprus and Paul taking Silas to Syria and Cilicia (Acts 15:36–41). Years later, Paul found Mark to be "useful" to him (2 Tim. 4:11), and, according to early church history, Mark spent a great deal of time with Peter and was endeared to him. The fact that Peter calls Mark his "son" supports this.

"Greet one another with a kiss of love" (5:14)—similar to Paul's own exhortations (Rom. 16:16, 1 Cor. 16:20, 2 Cor. 13:12, and 1 Thess. 5:26). We are not to merely "kiss" one another as a form of greeting; instead, the kiss is always modified as "a holy kiss" or, as here, "a kiss of love." Rather than Peter or Paul dogmatically imposing *kissing* as a means of greeting one another (a practice already in place when they wrote), the emphasis here is to greet one another in a *sincere, unhypocritical,* and *authentic manner.* Whether this greeting is with a kiss, handshake, hug, bow, smile and a nod, tip of the hat, fist bump, or whatever else, the *character* of that greeting must be "holy" and "of love." In other words, it is not to be like Joab's treacherous greeting of Amasa (2 Sam. 20:8–12) or the unholy and unloving kiss of Judas (Luke 22:47–48).

"Peace…in Christ" is not an empty or trifle expression but implies that our common faith in Christ is also the source of peace with one another. It is Christ's blood, doctrine, and fellowship that unites us all as brothers and sisters in the Lord. All other unities are solely of men or something far worse (cf. 1 Cor. 10:20, 2 Cor. 6:14–16, and James 4:4).

---

172 For a fuller evaluation of this, see R. P. Martin, "Mark, John," *ISBE* (electronic).

Introduction to 2 *Peter*

Much has been written about the authenticity of the epistle known to us as *2 Peter*. Prior to the final compilation of the NT, *2 Peter* (along with *James, Hebrews, 2 & 3 John, Jude,* and *Revelation*) was classified with the *antilegomena* [lit., to speak against] writings.[173] The epistle of *Jude*, while originally under suspicion, actually provides support for the authenticity of *2 Peter*, having several common subjects, and even an allusion from one to the other (compare, for example, 2 Peter 3:3–5 and Jude 1:17–18).[174] The implication is: either both letters are frauds, or both are legitimate. The evidence weighs heavily toward the latter.

This is not to suggest that we should accept *2 Peter* as genuine only because it is in our modern Bibles. Rather, an epistle like *2 Peter*—one of the most disputed books of the NT—must be either accepted or rejected based upon internal and external evidence, which determines its canonicity. "Canonicity" refers to the authentic standard (or, canon) of inspired writings supported by apostolic teaching, versus a rogue author who thinks he has something important to say. The internal evidence refers to the content of the material—what Paul calls "sound doctrine" (Titus 1:9)—that *must* be consistent with apostolic teachings elsewhere *and* the authoritative teachings of Christ. Unfortunately, the many instances of similarity between two writings are sometimes ignored only to focus on the differences.

External evidence is something other than (or outside of) the given work itself. The best kind of external support comes from those who are

---

173 JFB, *Commentary* (electronic), on "Introduction to 2 Peter." This is a very different classification than what are known as "spurious" books—e.g., "The Shepherd of Hermas," "The Revelation of Peter," "the Epistle of Barnabas," and, most recently, "The Gospel According to Judas"—that are outright rejected by all reputable scholars and Bible critics.

174 For more discussion on the relationship between *2 Peter* and *Jude,* I recommend my *1–2–3 John and Jude Commentary* (Spiritbuilding Publishers, 2024); go to www.spiritbuilding.com/chad.

closer in time, circumstances, and/or relationship to the author and his given work. On this, A. T. Robertson says of *2 Peter*:

> It was accepted in the canon by the council at Laodicea (372) and at Carthage (397). Jerome accepted it for the Vulgate, though it was absent from the Peshito [*sic*] Syriac Version. Eusebius placed it among the disputed books, while Origen [early 3rd century] was inclined to accept it. Clement of Alexandria accepted it and apparently wrote a commentary on it. It is probable that the so–called Apocalypse of Peter (early second century) used it and the Epistle of Jude either used it or 2 Peter used Jude. There are undoubted allusions also to phrases in 2 Peter in Aristides, Justin Martyr, Irenaeus, Ignatius, Clement of Rome. When one considers the brevity of the Epistle, the use of it is really as strong as one can expect. Athanasius and Augustine accepted it as genuine, as did Luther, while Calvin doubted and Erasmus rejected it. It may be said for it that it won its way under criticism and was not accepted blindly.[175]

It is true, however, that the early church seemed late (some say *reluctant*) to accept *2 Peter* as canonical. Some scholars also point to the fact that Peter cites John's gospel (compare 1:14 and John 21:18–19), and John's gospel was not written until the late first century (long after Peter was dead), and therefore Peter did not write *2 Peter*. This assumes, of course, that Peter—who was personally present for the same event that John recorded—could only mention something historical if already written by someone else (!). Such logic is presumptive and unfounded; yet it is examples like this to which critics of the genuineness of *2 Peter* cling.

---

175 Robertson, *Word Pictures* (electronic), in "By Way of Introduction" to *2 Peter*; bracketed words are mine. Kistemaker cites similar sources and conclusions in his commentary (*NTC*, 231). In the caves at Qumran, where the Dead Sea scrolls were found, there is a fragment of *2 Peter* attached as an introduction to the gospel of *Mark*. This cave was closed in AD 68, at the time the Jewish Wars against Rome began. If genuine, this would be the earliest attestation of the writing of *2 Peter* (Michael Green, *Tyndale New Testament Commentary: 2 Peter and Jude* [Grand Rapids: Wm. Eerdmans Publishing Co., 1987], 16–17). See also detailed quotes of the early church writers in B. C. Caffin, "2 Peter," *Pulpit Commentary* (vol. 22), i–iv.

Next, some scholars cite the variation of words between *1 & 2 Peter*: there are numerous words in *1 Peter* that are not used in *2 Peter*, and vice versa.[176] Yet, we have established the very likely idea in the Introduction to *1 Peter* that Silvanus was employed as the writer of *1 Peter*, it having been dictated to him by the apostle. If *2 Peter* used a different secretary (or *amanuensis*), then we should expect different vocabulary and other stylistic differences. Early church "fathers" wrote that Peter did use other men to help him with his writings.[177] Also, when the subject matter is radically different, writers tend to use a different vocabulary base. While some Bible critics are unhappy with this, it is, by itself, not enough to disqualify a single author for both letters.[178] In fact, a fair and objective comparison of *1 Peter* and *2 Peter* show far more agreement than not. "It would seem, in view of all this, that the ancients were not unreasonable in their failure to discern any fatal difference of thought and teaching between the First and Second Epistles of Peter."[179]

---

176 This same charge is made toward *2 Timothy* when compared to *1 Timothy*, or even *1 & 2 Timothy* when compared to, say, *Galatians* or *1 Thessalonians*. The idea among some scholars, especially more liberal–minded ones, is that they (the scholars) are the only ones who can determine correctly which words can or cannot be used by a given writer. If a writer uses a word they did not expect, or a phrase they think ought not to be known to the author, then that work must be questionable (!). This is a very subjective way to authenticate anything, yet it often hides under the cover of seminary–level scholarship, academic degrees (DD, DTh, LittD, etc.), and high–level publications. Green, on the other hand, provides scholarly evidence of more similarity between *1 Peter* and *2 Peter* than between *1 Peter* and any other NT book (Green, *TNTC*, 18–19).

177 Papias (early 2nd century) said that Mark was Peter's interpreter; Clement of Alexandria (late 2nd century) said that a man named Glaucias also helped Peter with his writings (Kistemaker, *NTC*, 217).

178 My theory, for what it is worth, is that modern scholars reject *2 Peter* not because there is so much evidence against it, but that they do not like what it says—namely, concerning the fiery destruction of the world. Those who subscribe to any form of Premillennialism, for example, are unable to reconcile the *absolute* and *final* destruction of the physical universe with their claim that the world will simply be *purged* or *purified* of human corruption, then rejuvenated, and then re–inhabited eternally by all the saved (except for the privileged 144,000 who, they maintain, get to live in heaven with God). The easiest way to get rid of teachings to the contrary of this doctrine is to undermine the credibility of their source material.

179 Green, *TNTC*, 23. Green—a capable scholar in his own right and who has certainly done his homework on this subject, later says: "[If] I am inclined to maintain

Purpose and Theme: Again, critics of *2 Peter* question, doubt, and even dismiss it as a genuine work of the apostle Peter because its content, style, and character do not seem to match that of *1 Peter*.[180] *Second Peter* is a different kind of letter altogether, but this is no reason to doubt its integrity. It is a letter of encouragement, but far more so a letter of warning. In the first epistle, Peter strongly encourages his readers to be submissive, remain faithful under persecution, and suffer for what is right. The second epistle serves as a *reminder* to be faithful, but also condemns false prophets and "mockers" of God's judgment; (twice) condemns the moral errors of "unprincipled men"; and describes the fiery judgment itself. The contents of these two letters will demand different approaches and different word choices.

Peter wrote *2 Peter* to Christians who remain unidentified, and thus the epistle falls into the category of "general epistles." There are no geographical references as we find in the first epistle (1 Peter 1:1).

---

its Petrine authorship, it is because I remain unconvinced by the arguments brought against it…" (*ibid.*, 38).

180 Barclay says: "There is no mention of the Passion [Jesus' crucifixion], the Resurrection and the Ascension of Jesus Christ; no mention of the Church as the true Israel; no mention of that faith which is undefeatable hope and trust combined; no mention of the Holy Spirit, of prayer, of baptism; and none of that passionate desire to call men to the supreme example of Jesus Christ" (*Letters*, 338). This is a very unfair criticism. First, Barclay arbitrarily chooses what he expects in a letter from Peter, and when Peter does not deliver, he dismisses the letter as ungenuine. Second, there are other NT letters that do not have all these subjects; if we applied his criteria to, say, *Philemon*, it also would fail the test. Third, this leaves no other recourse than that the letter is written by someone *other* than Peter, but who artificially *poses* as Peter—not once but several times (1:1, 14, and 16–18). Barclay tries to comfort us in this by saying "we must remember that in the ancient world this was a practice which was very common and quite normal" (*ibid.*, 341). Yet, Green rightly responds, "How is it that writers who urge the highest moral standards in their letters should stoop to deceit of this type?" (*TNTC*, 33). Lenski facetiously notes that if it *is* a forgery, it is "a forgery so well done that only Peter himself could have executed it" (*Interpretation*, 242). And the fact remains: if the apostle Peter did not write *2 Peter*, then we have no business reading it as a divinely revealed and apostolic letter. But the reasons for such dismissal are not, however, strong enough to warrant this; the letter's content do not contradict anything in the rest of the NT; and just because we cannot answer all the questions surrounding this letter does not render it spurious. (We have *many* questions about the books of the OT, for example, but this has not stopped us from accepting their canonicity.)

Rather, it is simply addressed to "those who have received a faith of the same kind as ours" (1:1); likely, "ours" refers to the apostles (see comments on 1:1). Peter says he is "ready to remind" his reading audience—Christians in general—of the things under discussion in the letter (1:12–13, 3:1). One of the motivations for writing may well be Peter's understanding that his life will soon end, as "our Lord Jesus Christ has made clear" to him (1:14–15; see John 21:18–19).

More specifically, Peter wants his readers to "be all the more diligent to make certain about His [God's] calling and choosing" them (1:10), and not to be distracted or grow lazy regarding their moral responsibilities. This requires personal diligence, an ever–increasing faith (1:5–7), being on guard (3:17), and growing in "grace and knowledge of our Lord and Savior Jesus Christ" (3:18). No doubt Peter sees things heating up against the church, the threat no longer merely being the Jews as in the beginning but increasingly the Roman government—a much greater and formidable enemy. His admonition, therefore, is to "pay attention" to the apostolic teaching so as not to be compromised by false teaching (1:19–21).

Peter's first epistle did not mention false teachers at all; his second epistle gives considerable attention to them. The first generation of Christians had been replaced by second and third generation believers whose convictions were not as deep or zealous as those who preceded them. Roman persecution would test the allegiance of all believers, but until then, Peter admonishes them to stay the course and "remember the words spoken beforehand by the holy prophets and the commandment of the Lord and Savior spoken by your apostles" (3:1–2).

Meanwhile, "false prophets" were attempting to infiltrate the church and undermine its stability, maligning the gospel and "secretly [introducing] destructive heresies" (2:1–2). He links the wickedness of men who distort apostolic teachings with the wicked people of Sodom and Gomorrah. Men who violate the natural laws of creation and those who violate the revealed laws of God are both regarded as "unprincipled" or lawless (2:7, 3:17). Peter goes into considerable detail—employing graphic and purposely–exaggerated language—as to the true nature of these false prophets (2:10b–19). Those who listen to such men and accept their false teaching put themselves in a hopeless situation (2:20–22).

One specific claim of the false prophets is that God's judgment against the ungodly world is, in effect, an empty promise, since "all continues just as it was from the beginning of creation" (3:4). This position ignores the actual details of Scripture, as Peter shows, and imposes upon God a very finite and human view of time (3:8). He goes on to affirm plainly that God's judgment most certainly *is* coming, the world *will* end, and the alleged "slowness" of such events has to do with God's patience in anticipation of people's repentance, not His inability to fulfill promises (3:9–12). Just as certain as is the end of the world, so is the creation of "new heavens and a new earth" for those who remain faithful to Him (3:13–14).

Finally, Peter warns his readers not to succumb to the error of "untaught and unstable" people who "distort" the apostolic writings "to their own destruction" (3:16). This likely refers to taking Paul's letters—since Peter specifically mentions these—out of context, or misapplying his teaching (on grace, the resurrection, Jews and Gentiles being equal in status in Christ, etc.) and creating an entirely new teaching which is different but lacks the power of the original (Gal. 1:6–9). Paul himself warned that people, to satisfy their own personal desires, will turn *away* from the truth and *toward* preachers who will accommodate them (2 Tim. 4:3–4). No doubt Peter is already seeing this and therefore giving his own strong warning concerning it.

Author and Date: This epistle opens with, "Simon Peter, a bond–servant and apostle of Jesus Christ" (1:1). Taken at face value, we know of no other Simon Peter than the well–known Peter whom the Lord chose to be one of His twelve disciples (Mat. 10:1–4) and to whom He gave "the keys of the kingdom of heaven" (Mat. 16:19). This means that either we accept Peter as the author up front—and therefore, whatever is said afterward is legitimate—or we reject Peter's authorship *and* this letter altogether. The book is either entirely real, having been penned by a genuine apostle of Christ, or has been penned by an impostor; there is no middle ground. "Whatever the motive for such a pious fraud, the fact remains that 2 Peter, if not genuine, has to take its place with this pseudonymous [lit., falsely authored] literature and can hardly be deemed worthy of a place in the New Testament. And yet there is no heresy in this Epistle, no startling new ideas that would lead one to use the name of Simon Peter. It is rather full of edifying and orthodox teaching."[181]

The fact is, the apostles, including Peter, were witnesses of Christ and heard His teachings; the author of *2 Peter* cites a specific instance of this in 1:16–18 (see Mat. 17:1–5 and 1 Peter 5:1). He also cites his brotherly relationship with the apostle Paul (2 Peter 3:15), which provides corroboration (just as Paul does with Peter in Gal. 2:6–9). He also talks about a fiery end–of–the–world event (2 Peter 3:10–12); Paul speaks of the same event, with very similar details (2 Thess. 1:6–9). Most notably, the author of *2 Peter* identifies himself in the salutation in a manner that we *should* expect, since this is how men identified him in the gospels (compare 2 Peter 1:1 and Mat. 16:16, John 6:68, 21:15, etc.).

This study maintains that the apostle Peter is most certainly the author of this epistle, and that there can be no serious alternative to this. As it stands, the burden of proof lies not with those who maintain Peter's authorship but those who insist otherwise. Unless or until someone can provide some proof in the other direction—namely, *positive* and *objective* evidence that this letter is indeed falsely ascribed to the apostle Peter—we can regard *2 Peter* as genuine and canonical. As such, it is "inspired by God and profitable for teaching, for reproof, for correction, for training in righteousness" (2 Tim. 3:16), as are all divinely revealed writings.

---

181 Robertson, *Word Pictures* (electronic), in "By Way of Introduction" to *2 Peter*; bracketed words are mine. Kistemaker adds: "Should a forger compose a letter in the name of an apostle, his epistle would be considered suspect and would be denied canonicity. The church rejected pseudonymous writings bearing Peter's name (for example, the Gospel of Peter, the Acts of Peter, the Teachings of Peter, and the Revelation of Peter) and regarded them as uninspired documents" (*NTC*, 218).

The date of writing cannot be determined conclusively, except to say (as mentioned earlier) that it is shortly before Peter's death. Roman persecution of the church began in AD mid–60s, and Paul was arrested and later executed because of it.[182] Peter also, according to tradition, was arrested and sentenced to death by crucifixion. The persistent tradition that he was crucified head downward (by his request, allegedly, because he felt unworthy to die in the exact same manner of Jesus) comes to us only through spurious writings, and therefore lacks substantiation.[183]

General Outline

- ❑ Salutation (1:1)
- ❑ Growing in Christian Virtue (1:2–9)
- ❑ A Needful Reminder (1:10–21)
- ❑ The Demise of False Prophets (2:1–22)
- ❑ The Promise of Christ's Coming (3:1–13)
- ❑ Closing Remarks (3:14–18)

---

182 Another criticism against Peter's authorship of *2 Peter* is his mention of Paul's letters (3:15–16). Allegedly, Paul's letters were not known as a collected work until late in the first century; thus, Peter's reference to them means "that this letter which is called *Second Peter* cannot have been written before that, and that, therefore, it cannot really be the work of Peter, who was martyred in the middle sixties of the century" (Barclay, *Letters*, 412). This conclusion assumes, of course, that the writings alluded to in the epistle were the exact same collected work of Paul's that, say, Barclay alludes to. There is no good reason to justify this conclusion. Several of Paul's letters were purposely circulated very soon after they were written (see Col. 4:16, for example); there is no need for *all* of them to be formally and entirely collected before Peter can refer to them.

183 Martin, "Peter," *ISBE* (electronic).

Salutation
(2 Peter 1:1)

The epistle's author identifies himself immediately as "Simon Peter, a bond–servant and apostle of Jesus Christ" (1:1), much as Paul has identified himself in a few of his own letters (Rom. 1:1, Phil. 1:1, and Titus 1:1).[184] (On "Simon Peter," see comments in "Introduction.") "Bond–servant" [Greek, *doulos*] is used metaphorically: indeed, Peter is a servant or slave of Jesus Christ, but he has bound himself voluntarily, and no one coerced him into servitude against his will.

Unlike the recipients of his first epistle (see 1 Peter 1:1), Peter did not identify the recipients of this letter geographically or otherwise. (However, they must *include* the recipients of the first letter, if Peter's remarks in 3:1 refer to 1 Peter: "This is ... the second letter I am writing to you.") He only identifies his readers as "those who have received a faith of the same kind [or, value] as ours"—i.e., Christians who have believed and obeyed the same gospel (thus, having the same faith) as Peter and the rest of the apostles. "Ours" is left unexplained or unidentified, but Peter (Acts 10:47) and John (1 John 1:1–3, 4:6) have used "we" and "us" to refer to the apostles, by implication, and it seems rather plausible to see Peter doing the same thing here (see comments on 1:16).

"By the righteousness of our God and Savior, Jesus Christ" indicates the saving power upon which such faith rests. Peter's bold admission that Jesus Christ is "our God and Savior" is conspicuous and most appropriate. (Remember Peter's earlier confession that Jesus *the Man* was also *the Christ* of prophecy and *the Son of God*—see Mat. 16:13–16. John confessed the same thing in John 20:31; Paul confessed the same thing in Col. 2:9–10 and Titus 2:13.) Being the Son of God means that Jesus is a divine member of the Godhead—thus, "God." The gospel

---

184 The old Hebrew spelling of "Symeon" is used in two early manuscripts, the Sinaiticus and Alexandrinus (Green, *TNTC*, 67).

accounts never question Christ's divine nature; only Jews who refused to accept His words and the miracles that accompanied them refused to believe this.

Growing in Christian Virtue
(2 Peter 1:2–9)

"Grace and peace" (1:2) is a common salutation among Christians in the first century (see comments on 1 Peter 1:2). Peter will end his letter with an encouragement to "grow in the grace and knowledge" (3:18), so that the two expressions serve as bookends to the entire epistle. The *content* of this knowledge is specific: it is not merely about religion, spiritual ideas, or a subject of personal intrigue, but "of God and of Jesus our Lord."

Magnificent Promises (1:3–4): God's divine power has bestowed upon believers everything they need for "life and godliness" (1:3). This does not mean God has given us miraculous knowledge or ability; there is nothing here to imply spiritual (miraculous) gifts. Rather, the divinely revealed word of God is all the information we need to benefit us in the most critical areas of our existence: *life* and *godliness*. In one sense, these are two separate subjects; in another, they are the same. Viewed separately, we might consider one's "life" in this world, including all things personal, interpersonal (relationships), secular, and mundane; one's "godliness" would have to do with his soul's welfare. Viewed together, "life and godliness" both hinge on each other: how one conducts himself in the world affects his spiritual welfare, and the disposition of one's soul before God affects his conduct in the world. Some see "life" as *spiritual* life, but one's spiritual life cannot be disconnected from one's *earthly* life, since it is our spirit that animates our physical body and allows for our conscious participation in the earthly realm.

Whatever contributes to "life and godliness" comes "through the true knowledge of Him who called us." In other words, knowledge of God increases one's growth, maturity, and perspective. (Compare this with Col. 1:9–10, where Paul prays for the Christians in Colossae to be "filled with the knowledge of His will in all spiritual wisdom and understanding.") Peter's emphasis on the word "true" indicates that there is knowledge in the world that is completely useless or even counterproductive to spiritual growth.[185] God's "divine power" is extended to those who are "called" (in 1 Peter 1:1, he uses the word "chosen"), that is, those who are in Christ and (by implication) who live faithfully with Him. It is not *our* calling upon God that is the source of our deliverance from sin; rather it is *His* having called *us* that means everything.[186] "Excellence" [Greek, *arete*] can also be translated "virtue," and is the same word used shortly regarding what we need to add to our faith (see comments on 1:5). It is *His (God's)* glory and excellence that provide us with true knowledge; such knowledge did not originate with people.

Through divinely revealed knowledge, God grants "precious and magnificent promises" (1:4). Peter emphasizes the great *worth* and *specialness* of these promises because they are literally priceless; we do not deserve them; God did not have to give them to us; no one else can give them to us; they cannot be found anywhere else; and *no one* outside

185 We know this by our own experience, and especially since the advent of the Information Age. We now have access to more knowledge and information than *anyone else in all human history*, yet people are increasingly oblivious to what knowledge is useful or beneficial. We might remember Jesus' own words, that some people pursue the "deep things of Satan" (Rev. 2:24), yet this is not only useless but hugely detrimental to their spiritual well-being. Just because one is knowledgeable, or has access to knowledge, does not automatically make him wise, or close to God, or in a saved condition.

186 We *must*, however, call upon God to be saved (Acts 2:21, Rom. 10:11–13, etc.). God calls us through His gospel (2 Thess. 2:13–14); we call upon God through our obedience to that gospel, visibly demonstrated in our baptism in water (Acts 22:16). The point here is: we could call upon God to save us all we want, but until or unless He calls *us*, nothing will happen. Similarly, we can have all the faith in the world in God's ability to save us, but until He provides His divine grace, nothing will happen. While we do—and must!—participate in our own salvation, the *power* of that salvation does not reside with us, but with Him.

of a covenant relationship with God through Christ can have them. Through a study of the gospel message, we know that these promises include divine mercy (Eph. 2:4); forgiveness of sins (Eph. 1:7); spiritual blessings (Eph. 1:3); spiritual strength (2 Tim. 2:1); access to God through His Holy Spirit (Eph. 2:18); access to God through prayer (Rom. 8:26–27); divine grace (Eph. 2:8), which refers to *anything* we need for salvation but cannot obtain on our own; and, most certainly, *eternal life with God* (Titus 3:7).

Having received these promises, we have communion with the Godhead—thus, we become "partakers of {the} divine nature" (1:4). "Partakers" [Greek, *koinonos*] means sharers, partners (in), or fellowshippers.[187] Divine *power* allows us to have fellowship with His divine *nature*. This "divine nature" refers not to God personally (although it *necessarily* implies this) but to His holiness, glory, and excellence (2 Cor. 7:1). This does not mean that we become divine ourselves—this is impossible—or that we cease to be human while having communion with God. It does mean, however, that we *do* have a spiritual relationship with God exclusive to those who are in Christ, and that this relationship—if we remain faithful to it—will continue perpetually, even eternally.

All this is only possible for those who have "escaped the corruption that is in the world by lust"—i.e., those rescued from Satan's domain of darkness and brought into God's realm of love, light, and holiness (see Acts 26:15–18 and Col. 1:13–14). "The world" refers to the realm of unconverted men, which is corrupted (or, in a state of perishing) with sin, and particularly "lust." This word "lust" [Greek, *epithumia*], in its neutral sense, simply means a strong desire, passionate longing, or deep craving.[188] Jesus used it with reference to His strong desire to partake of His last supper with His disciples (Luke 22:15). In its negative sense, it refers to a carnal longing for what is wicked and thus forbidden. (Whether "lust" is the *cause* of this corruption, or characterizes the *sphere* in which the corruption exists, is not clear, yet both senses apply

---

187 Strong, *Dictionary* (electronic), G2844.

188 *Ibid.*, G1939.

here.[189])

Supplying Our Faith (1:5–7): Since we have once escaped the world's corruption—and yet we continue to *live* in a corrupted world, and are thus continually assaulted by its sensual lusts, various temptations, and wicked people—we must guard against succumbing to that corruption again (1:5–7). The implication here is that our "escape" remains contingent upon our *faithfulness* to the One who rescued us. The ability to fall from grace is real, otherwise there would be no need to defend against it; the effect of falling from grace is disastrous (see 2:20–22). Grace and deliverance are what God supplies for our salvation; diligence and faith are what *we* must supply.[190] "Diligence" implies two things: earnest effort *and* a sense of urgent attention (Rom. 12:11, Eph. 4:3, 1 Thess. 5:12, etc.). It also implies efficiency and effectiveness, without which "diligence" amounts to little productivity. "In your faith" provides the context in which the believer makes such diligent additions.

Virtue refers to any morally excellent quality that imitates God's holy nature. Peter does not list the following seven virtues (1:5–7) in sequential order, that is, first add this, then this, then the other, and so on. Rather, we are to strive to always add *all* these virtues to our faith. Measurable progress should be evident over time as each virtue receives its due attention. Specifically, these seven virtues are:

❑ **moral excellence** (1:5). This can also be translated "virtue" (as in 1:3), and again describes any divine quality that is reproduced in believers. In classical Greek, (moral) excellence referred to manliness, manly courage, and the willingness to do what is right

---

189 Vincent, *Word Studies* (electronic), on 1:4.

190 "Supply [or, add]" is from the Greek, *epichorego*, "a vivid metaphor drawn from the Athenian drama festivals, in which a rich individual, called the *choregos*, since he paid the expenses of the chorus, joined with the poet and the state in putting on the plays. This could be an expensive business, and yet *choragi* vied with one another in the generosity of their equipment and training of the choruses. Thus, the word came to mean generous and costly co-operation. The Christian must engage in this sort of co-operation with God in the production of a Christian life which is a credit to him" (Green, *TNTC*, 76).

simply because it *is* right, regardless of consequences.[191] A faith
that will not do what is right is weak and ineffective; the pursuit of
righteousness necessarily requires a strong belief in God.

❏ **knowledge** (1:5). As stated earlier, this does not refer to any
knowledge, but that which comes from God's revealed word. One
can hardly have faith in God—or an ever-*deepening* faith in Him—
without knowledge of who He is and what His will is, as expressed in
Scripture (Eph. 5:17).

❏ **self–control** (1:6). This refers to one's mastery over his own
thoughts, actions, and convictions (Gal. 5:23, Titus 1:8). The KJV
uses the word "temperance" here, which is not a reference to one's
limitation of alcohol but to self–management/–mastery.

❏ **perseverance** (1:6). The English word "perseverance" is from a
Latin compound: "per–" (through) + "severity" (difficulty); thus,
the patient endurance of some arduous trial of faith (James 1:2–4,
5:10–11, Heb. 10:36, etc.). The Greek word here [*hupomone*]
can also be translated "steadfastness" or simply "patience," which
implies a cheerful staying power (as in, to stay the course in hopeful
anticipation of finishing it). This does not mean, "Waiting for the
inevitable," for even faithless people can do this; rather, believers are
purposefully to endure the trials of the walk that they have chosen
above all other walks.[192]

❏ **godliness** (1:6). Scripture never refers to God Himself as "godly"
(i.e., adjectively), for this would imply that He is reflecting a
character of something outside of Himself. But His faithful servants
are "godly," and what they practice is "godliness"—the virtuous,
pious, and supreme qualities that they learned *from* God. The
Christian faith must be one that reflects God's piety and holiness;
otherwise, it is something other than a godly faith.

❏ **brotherly kindness** (1:7). In the Greek, this two–word phrase
comes from a single word [*philadelphia*], which means "love of (the)
brothers."[193] "Brothers" here has a specific context: it refers only to

---

191 JFB, *Commentary* (electronic), on 1:5; see also T. L. Donaldson, "Virtue," *ISBE*
(electronic).

192 Adapted from Vincent, *Word Studies* (electronic), on 1:6.

193 Strong, *Dictionary* (electronic), G5360.

fellow Christians ("brethren," as in Heb. 13:1). "The insistence that all men are children of God simply by virtue of creation tends to depreciate or even obliterate the distinctiveness of *philadelphia*. All are indeed the offspring of God (Acts 17:28) and by virtue of that fact can be regarded as potential children of God, but the new birth is necessary for this to become a reality (John 1:12–13)."[194] One who claims to love God but refuses—for any reason—to show godly love to fellow believers has a corrupted view of what his faith ought to look like (see John 13:34–35 and 1 John 4:20–21).

❑ **love** (1:7). "Love" [Greek, *agape*] in the context of the gospel of Christ, always refers to *godly* love—a love modeled after nothing less than the divine qualities we see in God Himself (1 Cor. 13:4–7). "God is love" (1 John 4:8), and those who claim to be *of* God must therefore express His *kind* of love in their faith (1 John 5:1–3). Love is not the last thing to "add" to one's faith but is the binding agent *of* the Christian faith (Eph. 4:2–3, Col. 2:2, and 3:14): love is what makes our faith *work* and makes it *real*.

The Need for Ever–Increasing Faith (1:8–9): "For if these qualities are yours and are increasing …" (1:8)—this is a conditional statement ("if … then"). Conditional statements are always built upon a *premise* ("if") that is followed by a *promise* ("then"). The promise can only be fulfilled when its premise is honored or fulfilled; otherwise, there is no reason to anticipate it. Thus, *if* one diligently adds to his faith all these qualities *and if* they are steadily increasing over time, *then* he can reap the benefits of having fulfilled what God desired of him in the first place. Such regular, consistent, and diligent additions (improvements) to one's faith will be useful and fruitful—i.e., he will only continue to draw closer to God and become more grounded in his relationship with Christ.

But if he does *not* add these qualities to his faith, the Christian becomes spiritually "blind" or "short–sighted"—that is, he fails to see what God *expected* of him as well as the benefits He *offered* him (1:9). "Short–sighted" is from Greek *muopazo*, from which we get "myopia" for near–sightedness; it can also refer to a person who is squinting (shut)

---

194 E. F. Harrison, "Brotherly love," *ISBE* (electronic).

his eyes.[195] Regardless, Peter describes a person who fails to see the big picture of the spiritual world in which he participates. Specifically, he has forgotten what it took to atone for his sins, redeem his soul, and grant him priceless promises.

A Needful Reminder
(2 Peter 1:10–21)

Anticipating Our Entrance into the Kingdom (1:10–11): Since the possibility of failure always exists (recall 1:8–9), the believer must "be all the more diligent"—i.e., not easing up, but pressing forward, steadfast, and careful—to keep his faith healthy (1:10). "His calling" and "[His] choosing you" refer to a divine summons to live eternally with God the Creator—an invitation that must not be taken lightly. If the believer continues to do *his* part, God guarantees to do *His* part: "for as long as *you practice* these things…" (emphasis added). "Never stumble" cannot mean "never sin," because this is an impossible request. Our salvation does not depend upon flawless performance, but we are not to *practice* sin and thus be *enslaved* to it (Rom. 6:10–11, 1 John 3:6–8, etc.). The "stumbling" Peter has in mind, then, is not merely "sinning," but *falling from one's faith altogether.*

Peter's words are not meant to dismay but to encourage: "the entrance into the eternal kingdom" is indeed obtainable—by God's grace and through faith (1:11).[196] Many Christians think the church and the kingdom are interchangeable, yet we cannot be *in* one (1 Cor. 12:12–13) and *anticipate entrance into* the other if indeed they are both the same thing (Acts 14:22, 1 Cor. 6:9, 2 Tim. 4:18, etc.). It is far more accurate to say that the two things are very much related—the church *needs* the kingdom, and the kingdom will be given *to* the glorified church—but

---

195 Robertson, *Word Pictures* (electronic), on 1:9.

196 "Despite the amount of emphasis Peter has been laying on the need for growth, perseverance and effort in the Christian life, the concluding verses of this section (vv. 10–11) make it abundantly plain the 'final salvation is not man's achievement but the gift of God's lavish generosity' (Bauckham)" (Green, *TNTC*, 84).

not equal. We are "in the kingdom" *now* in a promissory sense, just as we are "saved" in the same way. No one is yet saved absolutely, for then we would not need to live by faith; likewise, no one has yet received the kingdom, for Christ's church has not yet entered eternal glory (Rev. 19:7–9, 21:1–5). But all who have been baptized into Christ *are now* in His church, and thus are "in the kingdom" by presently living in fellowship with the King.

In the NT, "kingdom" is most often referred to as *God's* kingdom ("the kingdom of God"—Mark 1:15); here, however, it is clearly stated as that which belongs to *Jesus Christ*. This presents no contradiction, since God the Father owns the kingdom and has inherent authority over it but has made His Son to be King over it for the purpose of redeeming human souls (Acts 5:31). The Father, however, remains exempt from being in subjection to His Son (1 Cor. 15:27–28). "Abundantly [or, richly] supplied to you" indicates a lavish amount of divine help in achieving this otherwise impossible goal. God is not helping us a little bit but far "beyond all that we ask or think, according to the power that works within us" (Eph. 3:20). Thus, we must not be doubtful about whether it is possible to be saved because God guarantees this if we remain faithful to Him.

The Truth Bears Repeating (1:12–15): Peter readily and encouragingly reminds us of that which contributes to our spiritual success (1:12). Reminders and deliberate repetition in teaching are a good thing. There is good reason, for example, for partaking in the Lord's Supper once a week versus sporadically (or not at all). Pulpit sermons seldom reveal never–before–heard truths to those who hear them, but most often are reminders to those who have become forgetful, distracted, or careless toward their commitment to the Lord. The original readers of this epistle were already "established [or, strengthened] in the truth"; this truth was "present with" them; yet Peter wishes to make them even stronger. This can only happen by (first) *not forgetting* God's teaching and (second) *actively implementing* that teaching in the form of godly living.

But Peter can only do so much, and he will only be in his "earthly dwelling [lit., tent or tabernacle]" for so long (1:13). Our physical body is mortal, finite, and destined to die. Furthermore, it is not good to wish to live forever upon a sin-corrupted earth; it *is* good to anticipate an eternal life with God (2 Cor. 5:1). While he is still alive, then, Peter recognizes his duty to stimulate the brethren "by way of reminder"; he considers this not "a" right (as in, a privilege, although this is true, too), but the right thing to do (as in, what is fitting and appropriate in God's sight as a shepherd of His people—see John 21:15–17). "It often happens that the task of the preacher and the teacher is to say to men: 'Remember what you know, and be what you are.'"[197]

Peter knows he is about to die, and there remains only so much opportunity to remind fellow Christians of their duty to God (1:14).[198] Many have speculated that Peter knows all the details of his impending death. While Jesus' words to him (in John 21:18–19) certainly do imply a death that is against his own will (versus a natural death), and one that will "glorify God," there is no evidence that he knew *more* than this. In any case, Peter speaks candidly about what lies in his future: he is at the end of his life. "Imminent" means "at any moment," and is translated from a Greek word [*tachinos*] which means "shortly" or "swiftly."[199] He believes that those to whom he is writing will recollect what he has taught them after his "departure" [Greek, *exodos*] from this life (see "departure" or "exodus" in Luke 9:31).

An Eyewitness of Glory (1:16–21): Peter now takes a moment to underscore his credentials as a spokesman for the teachings of God (1:16–19). As with "ours" in 1:1, so the three "we" pronouns here (1:16) refer generally to the twelve apostles. Specifically, they refer to Peter, James, and John—the three apostles who accompanied Jesus upon

---

197 Barclay, *Letters*, 363.

198 "We have much to learn (in our generation, when death has replaced sex as the forbidden subject) from Peter's attitude to death. He had for years been living with death; he knew that his lot would be to die in a horrible and painful way. And yet he can speak of it in this wonderful way, apparently without fear or regret. It means entry into the everlasting kingdom. It means the exit from this world (v. 15) to some other place prepared for us by God. It means the laying aside of the tent we have been inhabiting [cf. 2 Cor. 5:1]" (Green, *TNTC*, 89).

199 Strong, *Dictionary* (electronic), G5031.

the mountain in Caesarea Philippi where He was transfigured before them (Mat. 17:1–8, Mark 9:2–8, and Luke 9:28–36). Peter assures his readers that the source of his testimony about Christ did not come from "cleverly devised tales"—stories, myths, or fables that were the product of human wisdom or imagination, or the "false words" of false prophets (see 2:3).

Peter may not have *personally* preached the gospel to his readers, but this message is based upon apostolic teaching that originated with him and Jesus' other apostles (see 3:1–2). People make up stories; Christ spoke with *power* and (thus) great *authority*; "For the kingdom of God does not consist in words but in power" (1 Cor. 4:20). Not only did Jesus show power and authority in His earthly ministry, but He will reveal Himself again with great power (2 Thess. 1:6–9; Peter will talk more about this "coming" [Greek, *parousia*] in 3:3–12).

Peter, James, and John were "eyewitnesses of His [Christ's] majesty" (i.e., during His transfiguration) on the mountain (1:16). "Eyewitness" here [Greek, *epoptes*] refers to an onlooker or spectator, which is the only role that these three men had in that event.[200] Peter leaves out the fact that he attempted to do more than merely observe, but that detail serves no purpose here. The purpose for Jesus' transfiguration was at least twofold. **First,** it was so He could receive "glory and honor from God the Father" (1:17–18)—honor that He deserved as His only begotten and obedient Son.[201] **Second,** it was so Peter, James, and John could be eyewitnesses *of* this glory, as a further testimony (beyond the teachings and miracles that Jesus produced) to His divine nature.

---

200 *Ibid.*, G2030.

201 Jesus' transfiguration, in which He was made to shine with unearthly brilliance, alludes to the cloud of glory that filled the tabernacle (Exod. 40:34–35) and Solomon's temple (1 Kings 8:10–11) at the dedication of both structures. The Jews called this glory *shekinah*— a word not found in the Hebrew Bible but only in non-biblical writings—which refers to God's presence, or the place where God dwells. The Jews in the intertestamental period (historically, between *Malachi* and *Matthew*) utilized the *shekinah* as an indirect way of referring to God among the heathens, since they (the Jews) thought the name of God too sacred to use in everyday conversation (W. A. van Gemeren, "Shekinah," *ISBE*).

To prove irrefutably that Jesus was indeed the Son of God, the Father Himself uttered these words in the hearing of the three apostles: "This is My Beloved Son with whom I am well–pleased." (This happened on only two other occasions: Jesus' baptism [Mat. 3:13–17] and just prior to Jesus' death [John 12:27–30].) God's own glory is "majestic," meaning excellent, sublime, or magnificent,[202] words that befit the supreme and sovereign Creator who is the source of all life, light, truth, and authority. Not only did Peter *see* the transfiguration, but he also *heard* the voice on the mountain.[203]

Based on such credible eyewitness and historical testimony, Peter now lands his point—in essence, "Since these things are true, you would do well to *listen* to the apostolic teaching" (1:19). There is no indication that his original readers were *not* listening, but it is clear (as revealed in 2:1–3 and 3:3ff) that others were *rejecting* this testimony for various reasons. The "prophetic word" simply refers to whatever God's prophets have revealed, and particularly what Christ's apostles have revealed. This "word" was not to be disregarded but was to be accepted as true and relevant (cf. 1 Thess. 5:20–22).

So then, "you do well to pay attention" to this, since it reveals the brilliant Light of God to a sinful and ignorant world—a "darkened place" (see John 1:4–9, 12:46, Rom. 1:21, 1 John 1:5–6, and 2:8).[204] The "morning star" refers to Jesus (Rev. 22:16); the dawning of the "day" thus refers—since Peter just mentioned His Second Coming (recall 1:16)—to the time of Jesus' cosmic revealing of Himself at some time in our future. Peter makes a contrast here: for now, we have the "lamp" of God's word—a brilliant light set against the worldly darkness—but a "day" is coming when all the darkness will be dispelled (destroyed)

---

202 Vincent, *Word Studies* (electronic), on 1:17.

203 This calls to mind Peter's first sermon to the Jews in Jerusalem, where he declared that the power of God's Holy Spirit was something that the people could "both see and hear" (Acts 2:33). To see *and* hear serves as a kind of double witness to an event, which is sufficient to confirm it as true (2 Cor. 13:1, 1 Tim. 5:19).

204 "The term translated 'dark place' is that which denotes a squalid, filthy, and dark dungeon, a fitting description of the condition which characterizes men without the light of truth" (Woods, *Commentary*, 160).

and there will no longer be a need for the lamp (consider Rev. 21:22–27, referring to the church in its heavenly glory). "In your hearts" does not reduce this to an emotional experience but a very personal one. For now, we must abide by the light of God's word; in due time, we will see the Word of God (Christ) in person and will no longer have to rely only on the testimony of other men (Rev. 1:7).

"But know this, first of all"—as a matter of first importance—that divine prophecy, when it has been revealed to men (God's mouthpieces), must be accepted as God's word (1:20–21). Rather than Peter saying, "Listen to *me*," as though he had any inherent authority of his own, he says, in essence, "Listen to what God *revealed* to me!" The traditional position on these verses says that no one can understand Scripture unless the Holy Spirit interprets it for him. Yet this is a most inaccurate conclusion and is subject to all kinds of abuse by so–called priests, clerics, and religious know–it–alls. What Peter means instead is: *all* Scripture that is *indeed* Scripture has originated with God, not men. Divine prophecy is not something that comes from men, nor is it filtered through human presumption (Gal. 1:11–12).[205] God's prophets simply spoke what they were told to say (1 Kings 22:14), whether they themselves understood it fully or even at all (recall 1 Peter 1:10–12).

"Scripture," in the form of doctrinal teaching, is what God reveals (or breathes out), not what men decree by their own authority (2 Tim. 3:16–17). "We can rely on Scripture because behind its human authors, God spoke. The prophets did not make up what they wrote. They did not arbitrarily unravel it."[206] Thus, prophecy—the accurate stating of divine truth, not merely the telling of the future—is not an act of human will, but divine will (1:21; see Heb. 1:1–2). "Moved" here means borne along, as though riding a mighty wind (the same Greek word for "rushing" in Acts 2:2).[207] Even though the words may

---

205 "Interpretation" comes from a Greek word [*epilusis*] which means "loosening, untying, as of hard knots of scripture" (Vincent, *Word Studies*, on 1:20).

206 Green, *TNTC*, 101.

207 JFB, *Commentary* (electronic), on 1:21.

be attributed to a human speaker, it is the Holy Spirit who provided the message.

The Demise of False Prophets
(2 Peter 2:1–22)

False Prophets Defined (2:1–3): In sharp contrast to men who spoke from God, inspired by the Holy Spirit (recall 1:21), there have always been and will always be *false* speakers who speak from their own wicked heart (2:1–3). Not everyone who claims to be a prophet is from God; Jesus Himself warned that false prophets would usher in the final demise of Jerusalem (Mat. 24:11, 24) and infiltrate the church (Mat. 7:15–20). Paul had to contend with false prophets who "[disguised] themselves as apostles of Christ" (2 Cor. 11:13). Finally, John warns us to "test the spirits" of men "to see whether they are from God, because many false prophets have gone out into the world" (1 John 4:1).

There is not much difference between a "false prophet" and a "false teacher": both claim to speak for God, one in his prophesying and the other in his teaching; both are impostors and frauds; both mislead people by maligning the truth; and both are equally condemned by God. God warned Israel that false prophets would arise (Deut. 13:1ff, 18:19–20), and indeed they did, and corrupted the hearts of the people (Jer. 6:13–14, 14:14, 23:32, Lam. 2:14, Ezek. 22:28, etc.). Peter makes it sound at first like false prophets *will* come (as if they had not *yet* come) (2:1), but this can also read, "If you haven't seen them yet, you most certainly will, since they are all around you."

Peter tells his Christian brethren how to identify these false teachers. **First,** they "will secretly introduce destructive heresies" (2:1). "Secretly" indicates their wicked intentions: to avoid exposure, they work behind the scenes, laying down false teachings alongside sound doctrine, and purposely blurring the lines between what is false and what is true. False teachers rarely do this in the company of spiritually strong and biblically knowledgeable people; they target the weak in faith, weak in conscience, and weak in knowledge. "Destructive [or, damnable] heresies" are opinions that masquerade as divinely revealed doctrine[208]; they are not only destructive in what they *do*, but also will be the reason for the destruction of those who *propagate* them (Phil. 3:19).

The **second** thing false teachers do is "[deny] the Master who bought them"—a phrase that can have several implications. This can mean that they denied the actual teachings of Christ; they denied (or, renounced) the fact of Christ's primary responsibility for their salvation (and preached instead a salvation of works); they denied Christ's divine nature (as the Son of God); or they denied the flesh–and–blood *reality* of Jesus (a teaching of Gnosticism, which separates Jesus the *Man* from Christ the *Son of God*). What captures our attention here is that these false teachers were once "bought [or, purchased]" by Christ (Acts 20:28, 1 Cor. 6:20, 7:23, and Rev. 5:9)—i.e., these are not men who had *always* taught falsely but had been baptized as genuine believers. Even so, at some point they were seduced by demonic influences to become what they are now.[209] Just as freely as one can embrace divine truth, so one can also freely embrace satanic error.

---

208 "Heresy" literally means "school," "party," "sect," or simply the teaching or opinion *of* a particular school, party, or sect (as in Acts 5:17, 15:5, 24:5, 26:5, and 28:22). "Within the Church itself the term had from the very first a pejorative nuance," as the NT writers connected it—as Peter does in 2 Peter 2:1—with the sectarian spirit that divides churches and poisons the minds of many Christians (G. W. Bromiley, "Heresy," *ISBE*). Modern heresies continue to plague the church today, and are readily evident in denominational churches, evangelical movements, and many extremist views wrongly associated with NT Christianity.

209 Calvinist commentators wrestle and squirm with passages that clearly say that someone was *bought* by the Master but then becomes *condemned* by that person's own ungodly decisions and actions. Calvinism teaches that the saved ("elect") cannot fall from grace, yet Peter clearly says that some *will*, forcing us to choose (easily, I hope) between Calvinism and actual NT teaching. "[John] Calvin does not accept this epistle as canonical; in his extensive commentary on the New Testament it is not treated. May this clause, perhaps, have been a reason for this omission?" (Lenski, *Interpretation*, 305; bracketed word is mine).

Sadly, false teachers enjoy great success; "many will follow" them (2:2). They attract attention by appealing to the carnal desires of men. "Sensuality" refers to vice, licentiousness, wantonness, and filthy behavior (recall 1 Peter 4:3; see Jude 1:4).[210] False teachers mix these practices with their false teaching; "False doctrine and immoral practice generally go together."[211] This unholy union denies the truth about Jesus, as well as what He taught and commissioned His apostles to teach. Since Christ is "the way, and the truth, and the life" (John 14:6), to deny Him is to deny "the way of truth." "Maligned" comes from the same Greek word [blasphemeo] from which we get "blaspheme"; it means to revile or speak evil of what is sacred to God (Isa. 52:5).[212]

By speaking evil of God's truth, false teachers malign, distort, and corrupt the integrity of that truth so that it becomes something *other* than "the truth." Their greed for attention (and, possibly, monetary compensation for their teaching) is what drives them to do this (2:3a); the fact that they "exploit [or, make merchandise of] you with false words" is irrelevant to them. The Greek word for "exploit" [emporeuomai, from which we get "emporium"] is often used to describe a business transaction—a trading, buying, and/or selling of goods.[213] Peter is saying that these false teachers are just "doing business," in a sense, by selling false teaching to unsuspecting souls for a profit.

Having described what these false teachers do, Peter now spells out their awful future (2:3b). The fact that "their judgment" is from "long ago" does not mean they were *individually predestined* to be damned, as Calvinism claims; rather, it simply means that this *class of people* has already been condemned (or, doomed to destruction by God),

---

210 Strong, *Dictionary* (electronic), G766.

211 JFB, *Commentary* (electronic), on 2:2.

212 Strong, *Dictionary* (electronic), G987.

213 Robertson, *Word Pictures* (electronic), on 2:3. "Peter employs the word *exploit* to portray the activities of these teachers. This is a term borrowed from the marketplace, where the merchant is interested in making a profit. The unwary buyer becomes an object of exploitation. Notice that Peter writes the personal pronoun *you* to tell the believers about the perfidious [i.e., treacherous, disloyal—CMS] scheme of these peddlers" (Kistemaker, *NTC*, 284).

and therefore anyone who chooses to be in this class of people will be condemned along with all the rest who have done the same. "Not idle" and "not asleep" indicate that, contrary to what might appear otherwise, God has not forgotten who these wicked people are and will hold them accountable for their sin. (Peter will pick up this thought again in 3:7.) Just because false teachers enjoy a measure of success in this life does not mean they will escape divine justice in the life to come.

Historical Examples of Judgment and Rescue (2:4–10a): "For if God did not spare angels when they sinned…" (2:4) begins a long and detailed description of God's judgment against ungodly beings— whether angels or men—from ancient times (2:4–19). (Peter's "if – then" scenario that begins in 2:4 is not resolved until 2:9.) All this is to underscore what has just been said in 2:3, namely, that the destruction of the ungodly is "not idle" and "not asleep." Those who had sinned in the past were condemned to die (as were those destroyed in the Flood) or are awaiting their final condemnation in "pits of darkness" (as in the case of fallen angels). Since this is true—and is a matter of biblical and historical record—there is no reason to think that things will be any different for those who choose to identify with such rebels today. Just because God does not act right away—or, according to human expectations—does not mean He *will not act at all.* The same is true, however, for the righteous: if God delivered righteous men in the past, then certainly He will deliver righteous men today. We must be careful not to dictate the *terms* of this deliverance, however. Whether God "saves" us in the physical sense is irrelevant; our chief concern ought to be the spiritual salvation He promises those who remain faithful to Him.

Peter provides three classic and historical examples to make his point: the punishment of angels when they sinned; the punishment of the sinful antediluvian (pre–Flood) world; and the punishment of sinful Sodom and Gomorrah. These examples descend from the greater (angels) to the lesser (citizens of Sodom and Gomorrah), or possibly from the greatest in number to the least in number. In other words, it did not matter whether a great number of heavenly angels or a small number of mere mortals sinned, God's punishment will most certainly be forthcoming. "Neither their [angels'] former rank, their dignity, nor their holiness, saved them from being thrust down to hell; and if God punished them so severely, then false teachers could not hope to escape."[214]

The Punishment of Angels (2:4): "Angels" are spiritual servants of God and ministers to the saints (Heb. 1:14). They are mentioned frequently in the NT (over 80 times) and do play a significant role in the relationship between God and this world. Heaven has an entire army (or "host") of angels that will accompany Christ when He returns (2 Thess. 1:7). Human beings are, for now, "a little while lower" in nature, power, and authority than angels (Heb. 2:7). Even though angels are the highest beings of God's creation, they were not spared their due punishment "when they sinned" (2:4; see Jude 1:6).

Peter's statement, however, seems to create more questions than it answers: When did angels sin—was it a very long time ago, or is this something that is still happening? How can angels sin? What sins did (or do) they commit? Why do some angels sin but others do not? (etc.) Peter seems to be implying a past occurrence, possibly an ancient revolt in heaven (Jude 1:6). Satan himself was one of these rebellious creatures; there is no reason to believe that God created Satan *as* Satan, but He created a beautiful and powerful angel that chose to defy God and thus became an adversary (which is the meaning of "Satan"). When Christ took His seat at the right hand of God, Satan and his fellow angels were cast out of God's presence (Rev. 12:7–9).

There remains many unanswered—and unanswerable—questions regarding Satan, fallen angels, and the spiritual realm in general. It seems best not to try to fill in the blanks of what Peter says, but to simply take his message at face value and glean from it what he intended for us to know. Thus, we know that angels whom God created for *one* purpose abandoned this and turned aside to something else—why, how, when, etc., we will never know in this life—and as a result, they lost all privilege they once had *as* angels. Their sin was not left unpunished; their fall

---

214 Barnes, *Barnes' Notes* (electronic), on 2:4; bracketed word is mine.

had serious and significant consequences. Regarding salvation, we do know that God "does not give help to angels, but He gives help to the descendant of Abraham" (Heb. 2:16). In other words, there is no plan of salvation for fallen angels, only for fallen people.[215]

But what became of these fallen creatures? Peter says—without explanation—they were "cast [or, thrust]" into "hell." The Greek word for "hell" here [*tartaroo*, "Tartarus"] is found nowhere else in the NT but is relatively common in ancient secular writings.[216] It has given rise to a tremendous amount of commentary, speculation, and bogus teachings. Its counterpart is likely the Jewish *Gehenna* (Mat. 5:22), the abyss (Luke 8:31), and the bottomless pit (Rev. 9:1–2).

> [Tartarus] in Greek mythology was the lower part, or abyss of hades, where the shades of the wicked were supposed to be imprisoned and tormented... It was regarded, commonly, as beneath the earth; as entered through the grave; as dark, dismal, gloomy; and as a place of punishment. ... The word here is one that properly refers to a place of punishment, since the whole argument relates to that, and since it cannot be pretended that the "angels that sinned" were removed to a place of happiness on account of their transgression. It must also refer to punishment in some other world than this, for there is no evidence that *this*

---

215 It is traditionally thought that angels that *fell* became the wicked demons that were allowed to afflict people during the time of Christ and the early church. For now, we do not have a better explanation than this. However, one nagging question to which there is no satisfactory answer is: why were some demons/fallen angels allowed to torment people during Christ's ministry, but others were cast down into a prison–like abyss, as Peter will go on to explain? My thought, for what it is worth, is this: Peter speaks *generally*, even figuratively, of the demise of fallen angels, not specifically or literally. In this view, demons were not cast into the abyss immediately, but ultimately, which would explain the demon's plea in Luke 8:31. We would do well not to force the "abyss/pit" reference too strongly, since what happens in the spiritual realm cannot be adequately explained in the physical realm. Regardless, in my opinion, there are problems with any explanation one puts forward, and the true answer will probably never be known in this life.

216 G. A. L., "Hell," *ISBE* (electronic).

world is made a place of punishment for fallen angels.[217]

There is no reason to believe that Peter's reference to "hell" refers to the eternal fire that will be the final destination for "the devil and his angels" (cf. Mat. 25:41; see also Rev. 19:20, 20:10, and 20:14–15). "Hell" [*Tartarus*], in this context, is simply a realm of containment or banishment into which angels are cast, not their ultimate demise. Jude describes this containment as having "eternal bonds under darkness for the judgment of the great day" (Jude 1:6), where "eternal" implies a kind of bondage from which such fallen angels will never escape, either while waiting for the "great day" of judgment or after it has occurred. Angels that sinned were "committed (or, delivered) to "pits of darkness"—apparently, specific realms of containment within "hell" [*Tartarus*] itself. "Reserved for judgment" can refer to nothing else in the NT context than the final judgment in which Satan *and* his fellow angels/demons will be destroyed—not annihilated, but divested of all power and dominion, while simultaneously undergoing unspeakable pain and torment. "Sin is already its own penalty; hell will be its full development."[218]

The Punishment of the Flood (2:5): The second case Peter introduces as part of his overall argument is God's punishment of early humankind in the Flood (2:5; see Gen. 6 – 8). What precipitated the Flood was the fact that "the Lord saw that the wickedness of man was great on the earth, and that every intent of the thoughts of his heart was only evil continually" (Gen. 6:5). Such widespread wickedness and impenitent people required divine punishment; God did not "spare" them, even though they were made "in His own image" (Gen. 1:27), just as He did not spare angels when they sinned. Noah, "a preacher [or, herald] of righteousness," and his family (his wife, three sons, and their wives— seven people) are mentioned to show that God *did* spare those who walked with Him (Gen. 6:8–9; see Heb. 11:7).[219] Peter regards the Flood

---

217 Barnes, *Barnes' Notes* (electronic), on 2:4; all emphases are his.

218 JFB, *Commentary* (electronic), on 2:9.

219 In some older translations, 2:5 reads: "but saved Noah the eighth person …" This indicates *first* of all that Noah's preservation was necessarily joined by seven others; and

as a matter of historical fact, not a myth, legend, or allegory; Jesus did the same thing (Mat. 24:38–39 and Luke 17:27). Just as the punishment itself was real, so was the reason for that punishment.

The Punishment of Sodom and Gomorrah (2:6–8): The third case Peter provides is God's destruction of Sodom and Gomorrah, wicked cities of an ancient Canaanite valley that is presumed to be buried under the southern end of the modern–day Dead Sea (2:6–8; see Jude 1:7).[220] Again, Peter speaks of the destruction of these cities as a matter of historical fact: this really happened, just as it was recorded (Gen. 19:24–29). Peter cites the reason for these cities' condemnation in three ways:

❑ The inhabitants lived **"ungodly lives"** (2:6)—a level of ungodliness that warranted a full destruction. Enormous sin practiced habitually and without conscience ruins a people. In the absence of remorse or repentance there is nothing left to save. Even when angels struck blind the men of Sodom, these men still made every effort to engage in sinful behavior (Gen. 19:4–11).

❑ **"the sensual conduct of unprincipled men"** (2:7)—i.e., the licentious and pleasure–driven conduct of men whose moral compass has been destroyed by wicked carnal lusts. "Unprincipled" is from Greek *athesmos*, lit., "without lawful action," or simply "lawless," "criminal," or filled with "debauchery."[221] Jude says that the men of Sodom and Gomorrah "indulged in gross immorality and went after strange flesh" (Jude 1:7)—"strange flesh" being described by Paul as the "unnatural" function of a man's "indecent acts" with another man, or a woman's "degrading passion" for another woman (Rom. 1:24–27). In other words, they defied the natural order of Creation—the God–ordained establishment of marriage, procreation, and family—and chose instead to allow depraved lusts to dictate their behavior.

---

second, that he being "the eighth" indicates a newness of life, power, and identity, as is often symbolized by the number eight in Scripture.

220 There were in fact five cities of the valley, Sodom and Gomorrah being the largest of them; the others were Admah, Zeboiim, and Zoar; see Gen. 10:19, 13:12, 14:8, and 19:28.

221 Strong, *Dictionary* (electronic), G113.

- **"lawless deeds"** (2:8)—where "lawless" [Greek, *anomos*] means "without law."[222] While similar to "unprincipled," this word is broader in application. Lawless men practice a lifestyle without moral or legal restraints; whatever feels good is what they do, regardless of any law, whether it be God's or man's. This is not only true regarding "sensual conduct," but for all conduct in all situations.

Lot (Abraham's nephew) chose to live among such people, being influenced by the well–watered pastures for his livestock rather than considering the negative effect these people would have on his soul (Gen. 13:7–13). As it was, he was "oppressed" by what he had to see and hear on a regular basis from the depraved citizens of the valley (2:7); he "felt his righteous soul tormented day after day by their lawless deeds" (2:8).[223] While Peter regards Lot as a "righteous man," there is no question that the immorality of Sodom and Gomorrah took its toll on his wife (Gen. 19:26), his sons–in–law (Gen. 19:14), and his daughters (Gen. 19:30–36). Even so, it remains true that God did rescue Lot from the cities of Sodom and Gomorrah; the fault for what happened afterward (especially regarding his wife and daughters) lies with those involved, not with God.

While the temptation of the righteous may seem inescapable, and the justice due false teachers may never seem to come, neither case is true (2:9). God knows *how* to rescue the righteous *and* execute divine justice against the unrighteous; in fact, He will not fail to do either one (Psalm 34:15–18, 1 Cor. 10:13). "Temptation" does not have to refer strictly to an enticement to commit a certain sinful act; it can also refer to any trial of one's faith that causes one to doubt seriously or even abandon what he knows to be true (James 1:2–4).

As for the unrighteous, they are kept "under punishment" as they await the "day of judgment." Whether this means they are *presently* enduring a form of punishment (as illustrated by the rich man's demise in Luke

---

222 *Ibid.*, G459.

223 In the Greek, the "torturing" of Lot's soul is not something the Sodomites did to him but is what he did to himself (by remaining in the company of wicked men and observing constantly their wicked behavior) (Lenski, *Interpretation*, 314–5). The ESV, for example, reads: "he was tormenting his righteous soul."

16:22–24) or experience a "terrifying *expectation* of judgment" (Heb. 10:27, emphasis added) is unclear from this passage.

Those who "indulge [or, go after] the flesh in its corrupt desires" and who "despise authority" will "especially" (or, most expectedly) face God's wrath (2:10a). This refers specifically to those who have just been described in the accounts of fallen angels, the Flood, and the destruction of Sodom and Gomorrah. While the modern world blindly chooses to accept homosexuality and other lawless (immoral) behaviors, this is no different—and no better—than what we see in these ancient examples. Therefore, the punishment for such careless and irresponsible decisions will also be no different. We should not mistake God's patience for indifference toward or approval of such things.

Description of False Prophets (2:10b–19): At this point (2:10b), Peter engages in a graphic yet poetic description of the false prophets/ teachers who, he has warned, will most certainly appear among the brethren (recall 2:1–3; compare Jude 1:8–13).[224] The characteristics of false prophets—*not* people who may be mistaken in what they teach in their striving to please God, but those who deliberately and maliciously malign the gospel—are as follows:

❑ **"Daring"** (2:10b)—i.e., bold, but not in a good or noble way. Presumptuous, and even conceited (see 1 Tim. 6:3–5), would be another way to express this.
❑ **"self–willed"** (2:10b) means that they worship their own carnal appetite (or "belly"), not the God of heaven (Rom. 16:18, Phil. 3:18–19). Self–will is the exact opposite of self–denial (Mat. 16:24).
❑ **"they do not tremble when they revile angelic majesties …"** (2:10b–11)—this is a manifestation of such men's daringness and self–will. They have no respect for law or government; they have contempt for anyone who would not agree with or is superior to them. Since they live *for* themselves, they are not afraid to blaspheme whatever is not *of* themselves. "Angelic majesties [or, celestial beings]" refers the far higher rank of angels over that of

---

224 For an exposition of this passage in *Jude*, I recommend my *1–2–3 John and Jude Commentary* (Spiritbuilding Publishing, 2024); go to www.spiritbuilding.com/chad.

mere men—those creatures of greater dignity and higher glory than humans. Angels that serve God honor what is right, good, and pure; false prophets are not only unconcerned for such things, but they are unconcerned for those that honor them. Angels, while greater in might than men, still defer to God; false prophets, who are far below the rank of angels, indulge in self–inflated egos. Likely, Peter is referring to the same thing that Jude details, namely, Satan's dispute with Michael the archangel over the body of Moses (compare Deut. 34:5–6 and Jude 1:9). Michael, though an archangel, did not exercise his personal authority against Satan, but invoked God's judgment on the matter. Likewise, an angel, though "greater in might and power" (2:11), will defer to God's judgment of a false prophet rather than condemn such a person himself. A false teacher, in sharp contrast, invokes his own authority as being sufficient to settle all matters.

- ❑ **"unreasoning animals …"** (2:12a)—Peter likens the nature of false prophets to that of brute animals that rely on survival instinct rather than show the intelligence and reasoning ability of a man made in God's image. Those who act like animals in their character deserve to be treated like animals; they have forfeited the respect and dignity due a God–fearing person. They not only bring destruction upon themselves (in the form of divine judgment) but they are to be regarded as dangerous and uncontrollable, just as many wild animals are. Eventually, God will destroy them just as savage animals are also fit to be destroyed when they threaten human survival (2:12c).

- ❑ **"reviling where they have no knowledge"** (2:12b)—or, speaking evil of things they do not understand; denouncing things that ought instead to be commended. Being "natural" and not "spiritual" in their thinking, they have no right to appraise spiritual things (1 Cor. 2:14).

- ❑ **"suffering wrong as the wages of doing wrong"** (2:13a)—or, simply, receiving the reward of unrighteousness. In his first epistle, Peter stated that it was acceptable to God to suffer for doing what is right in His sight, but that one who suffers for his own crimes deserves what he gets (1 Peter 2:20, 4:15–16). Thus, false prophets will receive great suffering in the life to come, but they have brought this upon themselves and therefore deserve what they get.

- **"They count it a pleasure to revel in the daytime"** (2:13b). Such men show no restraint or sense of decency; they also show no shame for their actions. Worldly men often practice their worldly deeds under the cover of darkness (1 Thess. 5:7); shameless false prophets show indiscretion at all hours of the day. Since the "passing pleasures of sin" (Heb. 11:25) is their real objective, they do not hesitate to pursue this regardless of what is going on or who is watching.

- **"They are stains and blemishes, reveling ... carouse with you"** (2:13c). "[False prophets] are like a dark spot on a pure garment, or like a deformity on an otherwise beautiful person. They are a scandal and disgrace to the Christian profession."[225] They like to revel (or sport themselves) in their false teaching by indulging in what that teaching allows them to do—i.e., act like ungodly and irresponsible people. Yet, while they attempt to deceive others, they also deceive themselves (see Gal. 6:3, Jude 1:12). "Carouse" might better be translated "feast together (with)," as the Greek word strongly implies.[226] There is an allusion here to the so–called "love–feasts" of the early church, similar to Christians' modern potluck/devotionals, in which Christians came together to partake of a (sumptuous) meal together and, ideally, encourage one another concerning spiritual matters.[227] (This is also what Paul likely refers to in 1 Cor. 11:20–22, which had not only gotten out of hand but was mistakenly substituted for the Lord's Supper.) Peter says that false prophets will show up at these love-feasts, but Christian love is far from their mind. Their intent is to please themselves and gratify their carnal desires.

- **"having eyes full of adultery ..."** (2:14a)—a graphic way of describing someone who, in his mind, undresses every woman he sees and imagines himself being intimate with her. This, especially during the love–feasts. Thus, Christian women become objects of sexual fantasies as these false teachers gaze upon them with barely restrained lust. It seems that "adultery" here is used in the most

---

225 Barnes, *Barnes' Notes* (electronic), on 2:13.
226 Vincent, *Word Studies* (electronic), on 2:13.
227 *Ibid.*

general sense, that is, referring to any kind of illicit sexual activity rather than that which would require either party to be married. These men cannot look upon women without sinning (Mat. 5:28).

- "enticing [or, beguiling; entrapping] unstable souls, having a heart trained in greed" (2:14b)—false prophets/teachers commonly prey upon weak, naïve, and gullible people, since these are most susceptible to their lies and give the least amount of resistance or confrontation. These teachers cunningly seduce their victims with false kindness, smooth words, and half–truths (Rom. 16:18). Their own greed—for attention, money, followers, and the thrill of the hunt—is what inspires them to do such things. "These men have schooled themselves in the desire for forbidden things."[228]

- "[they are] accursed children" (2:15a). Rather than "descendant of Abraham" (Heb. 2:16), "beloved children" (Eph. 5:1), or "children of light" (Eph. 5:8), false prophets are wicked, morally depraved, and "sons of disobedience" (Eph. 5:6). Just like the Jews who adopted a heart of Satan rather than a love for God (John 8:44–47), these men are also Satan's children and will join him in his destruction (Mat. 25:41).

- "forsaking the right way, they have gone astray" (2:15b)—the "right way" is often depicted as a straight and narrow path; anyone who abandons this way or path has gone astray (1 Cor. 12:2, 2 Cor. 11:3, 1 Tim. 6:21). Those who themselves have gone astray will most often try to lead others to follow them (Mark 13:22). To turn *toward* something false, one must turn *away* from the truth (2 Tim. 4:3–4).

- "having followed … Balaam … unrighteousness" (2:15c–16)—a biblical and historical reference to Balaam, the pagan diviner, whom Balak, the king of Moab, hired to curse Israel while the Israelites were camping in Moab before entering the Promised Land (see Num. 22 – 24). Thankfully, God prevented Balaam from doing this, and instead had him *bless* Israel on three separate occasions. God gave the voice of a man to Balaam's lowly donkey in order to restrain that prophet from saying anything other than what God told him to say (Num. 22:22–35)—a humiliating lesson, to be sure.[229] Even

---

228 Green, *TNTC*, 123.

229 "Modern readers inevitably question a donkey that talks. This was simply not an

so, all of this did not change Balaam's heart, for later he counseled Moab to corrupt the sons of Israel through sexual enticement and idolatry—two things that often go together (Num. 25:1–9, 31:16). Fittingly, Balaam was killed through God's divine vengeance against Moab (Num. 31:8), underscoring the entire point of Peter's present message. False prophets—whether in Peter's day or ours—ally themselves with men like Balaam, always seeking some financial reward for their wicked ministries, and thus can be expected to be destroyed just like Balaam was destroyed.

❑ **"These are springs [or, wells] without water and mists …"** (2:17a; see Jude 1:12–13). Springs (or wells) without water are useless: one expects to find *water* in them, which is necessary for life, but instead they find *nothing*. The need for water—and the disappointment of *not* finding it—was a common problem for travelers in ancient times.[230] "Mists [or, fog] driven by a storm" refers to the *appearance* of water (in the form of rain, and even accompanied by a storm), but no actual *presence* of water (which is much needed for crops). Thus, false prophets promise much, but cannot deliver; they talk a big talk, but there is no substance to their claims. They talk about salvation, but they can neither offer it nor do they have it themselves.

❑ **"the black [or, blackness of] darkness has been reserved"** for these false teachers (2:17b). This corresponds to the "outer darkness" of which Jesus spoke (Mat. 8:12, etc.), the end for all those who reject Christ as their Savior and choose instead to identify with the passing pleasures of this world. It is "reserved" for them in the sense that there is a predetermined end for all such people, just as there is for the devil and his angels (Mat. 25:41, 46).

❑ **"[they speak] arrogant words of vanity"** (2:18a)—an intentional redundancy: all arrogant words are vain; all vain words come from human arrogance. Such men are swollen with pride and speak as

---

issue in the first century; nobody would have been troubled by it. The Old Testament was not a problem to the early church. It was their datum [or, primary basis] point" (Green, *TNTC*, 125; bracketed words are mine). It is amazing to me that someone today will question a talking donkey—and dismiss the entire Bible because of it— but will wholly swallow Evolution's lie that life sprang accidentally, inexplicably, and *impossibly* from non–living material, as well as many other lies.

230 Vincent, *Word Studies* (electronic), on 2:17.

if they know what they are talking about, but do not (as in 1 Tim. 1:6–7). Arrogant people often love to hear themselves talk and mistake their many words for intelligence and wisdom.

- ❏ **"they entice by fleshly desires, by sensuality"** (2:18b)—in other words, instead of producing honest, helpful, and life–giving words of hope, false prophets seduce unlearned people by appealing to their base desires, and especially their sensual pleasures (as in Rev. 2:20). The lust of the flesh is an extremely powerful force and will easily ensnare people who give attention to it. False prophets simply take advantage of this for their own means, thus holding such people captive to their own carnal desires—all of this under the masquerade of godly religion.

- ❏ **"[they entice] those who barely escape from the ones who live in error"** (2:18c)—likely meaning: some who seek the gospel as a means of escape from their error will be overcome by the deceptive words of false teachers.[231] Barnes says: "This seems to me to accord with the design of the passage, and it certainly accords with what frequently occurs, that those who are addicted to habits of vice become apparently interested in religion, and abandon many of their evil practices, but are again allured by the seductive influences of sin, and relapse into their former habits."[232]

- ❏ **"promising them freedom ..."** (2:19a). This is the typical characteristic of those who malign sound doctrine to conform to their self–serving agenda: they promise to others freedom (from sin, guilt, condemnation, and hell) while they themselves will be no more saved than those to whom they have lied *about* salvation. They offer a false hope based upon a false rescue; they promise others what they themselves do not have. This is like a man who is dying from an incurable disease promising to save another man who is also dying from the same: both men are doomed.

---

231 There apparently is some question on the Greek word being used here (depending on which manuscript is consulted) as to whether "barely" or "really" is meant. Most translators and scholars side with "barely," and this seems to be the more natural sense of the passage as well, especially given what follows in the next few verses.

232 *Barnes' Notes* (electronic), on 2:18.

❑ **"for by what a man is overcome, by this he is enslaved"** (2:19b).[233]
Peter provides this as a truthful observation on the situation just
described—one that applies equally to the false prophet as well as
the one who gives serious attention to his words. The false prophet
has *himself* been deceived before he ever started deceiving others;
he *himself* had been overcome by "the corruption that is in the
world" (recall 1:4) before he began corrupting others with false
hope. Addiction is described as a form of "bondage to the rule of a
substance, activity, or state of mind, which then becomes the center
of life, defending itself from the truth so that even bad consequences
don't bring repentance, and leading to further estrangement from
God."[234] But addiction does not have to come in the form of drug or
alcohol dependency; *sin* becomes an addiction when it is practiced
over time and becomes the driving force behind how a person thinks
and lives his life. This enslavement always begins voluntarily—by
enticement, then experimentation, then escalation, and then an
inability to escape—and is nothing short of satanic in nature (2 Tim.
2:26).

Worse Than When They Started (2:20–22): Peter now explains more
of what he has just said (2:20–22). He is not talking here about people
who *thought* they had escaped the "defilements [or, stain; foulness]" of
the world, but those who had *indeed* done so; they had not *imagined*
themselves to be Christians but had *in fact* become Christians (cf. Heb.
6:4–6). They once had the *true* knowledge of Christ; they "knew" the
way of righteousness through a "full and accurate" understanding of it.[235]
Tragically, they allowed themselves to become re-entangled by the same
wicked clutches from which Christ had once rescued them.

---

233 This can also be translated: "for a man in enslaved to whatever has mastered him"
(Kistemaker, *NTC*, 309). "There is a counterpart to this NT teaching in Platonism and
Stoicism: persons who are legally free but controlled by their vices are really slaves;
those who are legally slaves but pursue goodness and truth are really free" (F. F. Bruce,
"Liberty," *ISBE*). Yet, no one can truly be free from *sin* apart from the mediatory work
of Christ: "Therefore there is now no condemnation for those who are in Christ Jesus"
(Rom. 8:1), and "It was for freedom that Christ set us free" (Gal 5:1).

234 Edward J. Welch, *Addictions: A Banquet in the Grave* (Phillipsburg, NJ: P & R Publ.
Co., 2001), 35.

235 JFB, *Commentary* (electronic), on 2:20.

And now, Peter says, "the last state has become worse for them than the first" (2:20). They came to Christ as dogs and swine; when they abandon Christ and relapse into their pre–converted state, they return to being dogs and swine, doing the disgusting things that dogs and swine do (2:21–22). Yet, now that they have returned to this awful state, they render themselves ineligible as candidates for salvation. They have deliberately and impenitently spit in the face of God, insulted the Holy Spirit, and trampled underfoot the holy blood of the Savior (Heb. 10:26–31). There remains for them no other gospel and no other hope..[236] Thus, it will be "better" (as in, judgment will be less severe) for those who had never made a commitment to the Lord in the first place than it will be for these re–fallen people. Peter quotes from Prov. 26:11 to underscore his point: "Like a dog that returns to its vomit is a fool who repeats his folly."

The Promise of Christ's Coming
(2 Peter 3:1–13)

Peter himself says that this epistle is the second one he has written (3:1–2), lending great credibility to both epistles.[237] His intent, as already

---

236 The question here is: who exactly *are* these people? Are they those who, upon successfully putting to death *one* sinful behavior, are now dealing with *another*? Or, those struggling to overcome addictive behavior, but stumble from time to time? Or, those going through a particularly dark and difficult time in their spiritual life? When we compare Peter's words with Heb. 6:4–6 and 10:26–31, it seems clear that both Peter and the *Hebrews* writer are talking about those who walk away (or apostate) from the gospel and all that it offers. Thus, they are not describing someone who is battling sin but one who has stopped fighting it altogether and gives himself wholly over to sin's corruptive effects. This does not mean, however, that those in the other scenarios I just described are completely out of danger, but that they can still be victorious over this world if they never stop striving to enter the kingdom of God (Luke 13:24). Paul's words are especially important here: "Do not be overcome by evil, but overcome evil with good" (Rom. 12:21).

237 This is true *if* the other letter referred to here is what we know as *1 Peter*, which we cannot know for certain. It is possible that it does not refer to *1 Peter*, but to a different

mentioned earlier (recall 1:13–14), is to provide a reminder to his readers of the things they need to hear from a chosen apostle of Christ. His full desire is to "stir up" their minds—i.e., to arouse their attention to what is really going on—so that they will not be uninformed or seduced by what he later refers to as "the error of unprincipled men" (3:17). The means by which to avoid being misinformed or misled is to remember what has already been taught.

"Remember" (3:2) does not mean merely to call to mind; it means to honor and obey (as in 2 Tim. 2:8 and Rev. 3:3). "Holy prophets" (3:2) were God's mouthpieces, uttering the prophecies and revealing the spiritual future of Israel as embodied in Christ and His church. The entire gospel of Christ is rooted in the OT prophecies, kept alive not only by the prophets themselves but also the faithful remnant of Israel (Luke 24:44–47, 1 Cor. 15:3–4 ["according to the Scriptures"]). "The commandment of the Lord and Savior" does not refer to any single command, but all of them. Whatever Christ told us to do is His "commandment." Christ first revealed this commandment; His apostles also revealed whatever He commissioned them to speak (Heb. 2:3b–4, 1 John 1:1–3, and Jude 1:17).

Mockers of God's Judgment (3:3–9): In their (and our) remembrance of these things, believers should not try to gauge the worthiness of what God has promised by how long it takes for this to be fulfilled. Peter has already alluded to Christ's Second Coming (recall 1:16); now he returns to the subject as a matter of serious consideration and something for which believers ought to be prepared.

"First of all," he says, it is a serious error to dismiss God's promise of Christ's coming and His judgment of the world simply because it has not yet happened (3:3). Peter calls such people "mockers"—scoffers, and, by implication, false teachers—in that they undermine or ridicule God's authority by holding Him hostage to their own short-sighted

letter written to the same audience to which this present letter has been addressed, a letter that may have "suffered the same fate of the majority of apostolic correspondence and been lost to posterity" (Green, *TNTC*, 135).

expectations (Jude 1:18). "Mockers … mocking" is intentionally redundant: not only *are* such men mockers (by definition), but they *act* like mockers (by what they say). The "last days" does not describe a time frame that already exists (as in Heb. 1:2) but one that has yet to come (as in 1 Tim. 4:1).

Mockers *will* mock, indicating future action; this does not mean they are not *already* mocking, but that they will think they have more *reason* to mock since so much time has passed (by then) and there is still no sign of Christ's return. Such men will not be giving serious attention to the prophecies but follow "their own lusts"—i.e., using their own pleasure as a standard for what seems true or real to them. Their cynicism breeds self-indulgence; "Their pleasure is their sole law, unrestrained by reverence for God."[238] Ironically, their mocking or scoffing will only confirm what Peter now says about them, thus fulfilling his own prophecy concerning them.

People have been wondering about, waiting for, and even questioning the reality of Christ's return for 2,000 years. Many have made predictions of this event, all of which have turned out to be false; this simply adds to the wonderment and discouragement of those who want Jesus to come in their lifetime. Adding to many people's fading hope of the prophecy of Jesus' return is the fact that the world continues to exist with no cataclysmic change—and no indication of a final ending (3:4).

The "fathers" here (3:4) refers to those to whom the promise was originally made, which includes Peter and the other apostles (Acts 1:9–11). However, the mockers' argument is not based upon God's power, His word's infallibility, or the record of God's divine judgment in the Bible. It rests entirely upon a human perception of the physical world—its laws, sciences, material composition, and natural expectations—which completely ignores God's *supremacy* over all such things. The

238 JFB, *Commentary* (electronic), on 3:3. "For men who live in the world of the relative, the claim that the relative will be ended by the absolute is nothing short of ludicrous. For men who nourish a belief in human self-determination and perfectibility, the very idea that we are accountable and dependent is a bitter pill to swallow. No wonder they mocked!" (Green, *TNTC*, 138).

Second Coming will be a miracle—a miracle seen by the entire world!—and *all* miracles, by definition, supersede all laws of nature and earthly expectations. The mockers, in essence, insinuate that God is no longer able to *be* God since He can no longer bring about a miracle by His own power.

Such mockers also assume—ignoring the OT record—that since "the beginning of creation" no cataclysmic judgment of God has affected the natural world (3:4b). Peter cites that which has "escaped their notice"—a polite way of saying, "They are stupid to believe otherwise"—regarding the creation of the world *and* God's judgment upon it (3:5–6). It was "by the word of God" that the heavens and earth *were* created (Gen. 1:2ff, Heb. 11:3); and it was "by the word of God" that the earth was submerged beneath the Flood. No doubt those who watched Noah build his ark also thought the world could *never* be destroyed by water because that had never happened before!

In both cases, water was the agent God used to carry out His will upon the earth. Water serves as an agent of birth—the world was in effect *born* out of water—as well as spiritual rebirth (John 3:3–5, 1 Peter 1:23). Water also serves as an agent of cleansing (Exod. 29:4, 30:18–21, Lev. 14:8–9, 16:26, etc.), the most extreme form of cleansing being the removal of all sinful men from the face of the earth (Gen. 6:12–13). In that case, "the world ... was destroyed"—a reference to all *life* upon earth (save those people and animals in the Noah's ark), not the physical system itself.[239] Thus, the world was buried *in* water and reborn *through* water, parallel to one's death to the "old" life in baptism and his resurrection to "newness of life" in Christ (Rom. 6:4).

Peter says that what God did once with water—i.e., bring judgment upon all humankind—He will do again with fire. The difference between

---

239 There are many who claim that the Genesis flood was a limited (geographically localized) event, that it only submerged a relatively small part of the world to destroy those who lived at that time. Yet, Peter speaks of the world being born out of water and destroyed by water in the same way. In other words, just as it was not only *part* of the world that was born, so it could not have been only *part* of the world that was destroyed.

water and fire as destroying agents is the level of destruction each one brings. Water can destroy human life, to be sure, and can certainly alter the face of the earth. But fire—if it is hot enough—destroys *anything*. Water destroys the structure of things, but fire destroys the very *form* of them. A flood can come against a house and destroy *the house*; but if fire comes against a house, it destroys not only the house but *everything of which the house was comprised*. Water can drown a person, reducing him to a corpse; fire will also kill a person, turning the corpse into its most primary elements.

Thus, "By His word the present heavens and earth are being reserved for fire" (3:7a). "Reserved" (stored up; treasured, as in Mat. 6:19) indicates that this event is already on God's schedule; it will not be an accidental or spontaneous action. God has been planning this for some time, and He is fully capable of making it happen. The same God who spoke the heavens and earth *into* existence can also speak them *out* of existence. The same God who birthed our world by water can certainly terminate our world by fire. This future conflagration serves as a "day of judgment and destruction of ungodly men" (3:7b). Peter gives no indication of the level of wickedness in the world on the day of its judgment, or how it will compare to what Noah faced in his day. He only says that this is what will happen, at a time of God's choosing, when all the conditions requiring such a destruction have been met.

This passage (3:7–12) implies that men will have so thoroughly corrupted the physical earth with sin that it must be burned up entirely to remove the effects of that corruption. The fiery destruction of Sodom and Gomorrah prefigures this cataclysmic event: those people so corrupted their land that the land *itself* had to be burned up. But more is involved than merely the destruction of the earth; "the present heavens" will be involved as well. Thus, whatever God created "in the beginning" (Gen. 1:1) will be destroyed *in the end*. There is no way to understand this contextually other than that the entire physical creation—earth, our sun, our galaxy, and our universe—will erupt in fire.[240] (Exactly *how* God

---

240 "The same Word that carried out the catastrophism of water is to carry out the catastrophism of fire" (R. Finlayson, "2 Peter," *Pulpit Commentary*, 86).

will do this does not need to be explained any more than how God spoke all these things into existence in the first place.) The apostle John, in the vision revealed to him, says of our future, "Then I saw a new heaven and a new earth; for the first heaven and the first earth passed away, and there is no longer any sea" (Rev. 21:1). What Peter predicts, John "saw"; both apostles "see" the same thing. John does not define what this *new* heaven and earth will look like, or whether it will be anything even resembling what we know now, but simply that God is "making *all* things new" (Rev. 21:5, emphasis added).[241]

Peter began this discussion with "Know this first of all" (recall 3:3), but now adds, "But do not let this one fact escape your notice [or, do not be ignorant of this one thing]" (3:8a). He wants his readers—including us—to pay close attention to what he is saying, and to consider the full picture rather than simply dwelling on one small part of it. Peter is still refuting the mockers/scoffers who argue that the great amount of time that has passed since the promise was made (of Christ's coming, which coincides with the destruction of the world) negates the promise itself. Yet God's *promise* of what will happen is as sure as the event's reality; because He is God, He cannot lie, He cannot forget, and His promise cannot fail.

God created physical time when He created the physical world; everything we *know* of time is measured by the physical creation (i.e., the rotation of the earth, its orbit around the sun, the change of seasons, and the visible aging of all material things). If there were no physical objects by which to measure time, then time would not exist (or would be irrelevant). Since God *created* time, He operates outside of it; He is not constrained by time but works independent of it. This does not mean He does not *use* time as a means of carrying out His will (see Rom. 5:6 and Gal. 4:4, for example), but that He is not *bound* by time and therefore it

_____

241 It is outside our present discussion, but John's detail that "there is no longer any sea" indicates that this "new earth" will not be made from water as our present earth was. In my opinion, I do not think John is talking about anything resembling the physical earth, not even a "spiritual" replication of it. He is speaking of a new *dwelling place* for the people of God—in other words, not a new physical universe, but an altogether new kind of existence.

does not matter how long or short of time it takes Him to do anything. God created the world in six days; He could have just as easily created it in six hours—or six minutes—if that is what He desired. Likewise, whether it takes two minutes or two thousand-plus years for Him to act, it makes no difference.

How long it takes for God's promise to be fulfilled depends upon two factors that are often outside of human ability to know: the *sequence* of necessary events to unfold (to usher in the promise) and/or the *conditions* that need to be fulfilled (to *require* the promise). Sequence of events indicates a certain order of things (1, 2, 3, … ; A, B, C, …); conditions refer to circumstances, stipulations, or situations. These factors may *include* time—e.g., sequences that happen *over time*, or the condition of a certain *passage* of time—but are not bound by time itself. God does not use our calendar; He does not need our clocks; He is not confined to our time-determined world; and He will not succumb to the effects of physical time. Thus, "one day is as a thousand years," and vice versa (3:8b)—just as God Himself is timeless, ageless, and lives in the ever-present "now," so His promises never falter, diminish, or fall off the grid, so to speak (Psalm 90:4). The mockers' argument that God's promises are nullified by time is completely unjustified.

Now Peter goes on the offensive, in a sense: instead of simply refuting the mockers' argument, he provides a superior one in its place: "The Lord is not slow [or, slack] about His promise…, but is patient toward you" (3:9a). The long duration between when the promise is given and when it is fulfilled is not due to God's slowness (a negative insinuation) but His merciful patience (a positive reason). There is no question that God will bring about the judgment of ungodly men, and thus the destruction of our sin–filled world, but He is not rushing to do this. "Patient" here means longsuffering, forbearing, or willing to bear a duration of *time* to bring about a desired result.[242] God's patience ought to be seen as opportunity for salvation (see 3:15), not inability to act. However, He will not wait forever: once people no longer response *to* His patience, then judgment will come. For now, He waits, continuing to shower us with physical blessings to get our attention and prick our

242 Strong, *Dictionary* (electronic), G3114.

hearts (Rom. 2:4). "You" here is not limited to Peter's reading audience but applies to *all* people of *any* generation.

"[God] desires all men to be saved and to come to the knowledge of the truth" (1 Tim. 2:4); thus, He does not "[wish] for any to perish but for all to come to repentance" (3:9b). Anyone who thinks that God does not care about his or her salvation needs to be confronted with these two verses.[243] God has *never* desired to bring about judgment against people *rather than* have them respond rightly to His love and grace and come to their senses. If God were not willing to save people, then it would be pointless for Him to extend patience toward them. "'Do I have any pleasure in the death of the wicked,' declares the Lord GOD, 'rather than that he should turn from his ways and live?'" (Ezek. 18:23).

All said, Peter has refuted the mockers' argument with three points:

- The world has *not* always remained unchanged: it was once completely flooded with water in an act of divine judgment against sinful men.
- The duration of earthly time is irrelevant to a timeless and transcendent God. Just as He is not part of the physical world (but is above it in every respect), so He is not bound to the passing of time as mortal men are.
- The fact that God has not yet destroyed the world with fire is not because He is *unable* to do so, or because this *cannot* happen, but only because God waits patiently for more people to repent of their wickedness and call upon Him for salvation.

The "Day of the Lord" (3:10–13): In the context of Christ's gospel, "the day of the Lord" (3:10a) cannot refer to anything but His Second

---

243 These verses also put a few more nails in the coffin of Calvinism, the man-made teaching that God has already predestined every *individual person* who will be saved, and thus … who will be lost. It is illogical—and unbiblical—for God to offer salvation to people who are *already* saved, or to those who *cannot* be saved. Once again, salvation is a choice: God desires all men to be saved, but not all men desire His salvation; on the other hand, whoever calls upon Him *for* salvation "will not be disappointed" (Rom. 10:11–13).

Coming.[244] Since its usage in the OT prophets, "day of the Lord" has always meant a time of great change, upheaval, or judgment. For believers, this "day" is a time of deliverance, vindication, and the ushering in of a new (and far better) age (as in Acts 2:14–21); for unbelievers, it is a "day" of fear, loss, ruin, and death (as symbolized in Rev. 6:12–17). When Jesus returns in the clouds, both of these will be evident: the righteous (living and dead) will be taken up to be with Him in glory forever (1 Thess. 4:13–18); the unrighteous will be destroyed along with the earth (2 Thess. 1:6–9), and then sentenced to the "outer darkness" where "there will be weeping and gnashing of teeth" (Mat. 8:11–12, 22:13, and 25:30). The fact that this "day...will come like a thief" means at least the following:

- It will come at a time when it is not expected (Luke 12:40, 46, and Rev. 3:3, both in principle).[245] Jesus gives the example of those in the days of Noah and the days of Lot who lived as if their world would go on indefinitely, and then were surprised by God's judgment (Mat. 24:38–39, Luke 17:26–29). So it will be in the *final* day, when the entire world will be unprepared for what comes upon it.
- No one will be able to predict exactly when this "day" *will* come. All those who attempt to do so either do not understand what coming "like a thief" means or think they are too clever to be taken by surprise.

---

244 I recommend my *1 & 2 Thessalonians Commentary* (Spiritbuilding Publishers, 2025) for a much fuller explanation on "the day of the Lord" and Christ's Second Coming; go to www.spiritbuilding.com/chad.

245 I say "in principle" because, in my understanding, these citations do not refer to the *final* day of the Lord (as in, the end of the world), but *a* day of the Lord (as in, judgment for a different reason, and toward a specific group of people). In Luke 12, as in virtually all His discourses to the Jews about judgment, Jesus is talking about what will soon happen (12:56), namely, the destruction of Jerusalem and the end of the Jewish system (AD 70). In Rev. 3:3, Jesus' promise of judgment to the churches is not actually aimed at them but the Roman Empire. However, He says to the church at Sardis (and others) that Christians who do not honor their covenant with Him will also be recipients of God's divine wrath toward Rome. There are, then, three different contexts for Jesus' "coming" in the NT: His "coming" against the Jewish nation (Mat. 24:29–31); His "coming" against the Roman Empire (Rev. 1:7, 22:7); and His "coming" at the end of the world (1 Thess. 3:13, 5:23, 2 Thess. 1:10, 2:1, etc.).

- It will happen suddenly, but not accidently or arbitrarily. God is omniscient and goal–oriented by nature; therefore, all His plans are carried out with full knowledge and on purpose.
- Those who take the appropriate measures to prepare for this day will not be overtaken by it (1 Thess. 5:2–4, Rev. 16:15). While believers cannot predict *when* Christ will come, this does not mean we should be *unprepared* for it (Mat. 25:1–13, in principle).
- Those who do *not* take such measures will suffer complete and irretrievable loss because of it. Once Christ comes, there will be no more opportunity for learning the gospel, repenting of sins, or being saved. At that time, every person will have already made the decision to live by faith in God or reject His offer of salvation.

First, Peter says *how* the "day of the Lord" will come: "like a thief." Now, he tells us what will *happen* when that "day" comes: "the heavens will pass away" and "the earth and its works will be burned up" (3:10b). There has been *much* written about this passage—too much, perhaps—because everyone seems to have their own idea of what this means. On many occasions, such writings are not as interested in extracting the truths of this passage as in defending a predetermined agenda. Thus, Preterists want this passage to say that the Jewish system and all *its* works (the Jewish temple, in particular) is what will be burned up.[246] Jehovah's Witnesses (and others) see this as the mere purging of the earth by fire to allow God to turn it into a revived and worldwide Garden of Eden. Premillennialists try to cram this into an alleged thousand–year (millennial) reign of Christ on the earth.

There is no good reason to believe that "the heavens" and "earth" are *different* than what God created in "the beginning" (Gen. 1:1).[247] In no other biblical "day of the Lord" context does it say that what God created in the beginning will be "destroyed" and "burned up" as Peter here

---

246 Sam Dawson, *II Peter 3: Destruction of Universe or Destruction of Jerusalem?* (Amarillo, TX: Gospel Themes Press, 1997).

247 To clarify: "the heavens," as used in or associated with the domain of human existence, has nothing to do with God's heaven, that is, the spiritual realm in which He dwells with Christ, His Holy Spirit, and all His angels.

describes. Thus, this destruction must be far greater in scope than all previous "days" of judgment, with different conclusions or consequences than what have been seen before. In God's word are revealed beginnings and endings to every subject that directly affects God's "eternal purpose which He carried out in Christ Jesus our Lord" (Eph. 3:11). Thus, God created man's world "in the beginning"; He will destroy man's world in the end: whatever He creates He can also destroy. "Heavens" (the cosmos) and "earth" are all part of the human world—i.e., whatever we can see and whatever is included in what we can see are part of Creation. Human souls are all that will survive the physical Creation since these are directly linked to God Himself and will continue to exist in the unseen spiritual realm.

This "day" that Peter describes has every characteristic of the *ultimate* "day of the Lord." Indeed, there is a profound sense of finality in this verse (3:10), giving no opportunity for or any indication of another "day" like it, especially in the earthly context.

❑ **"the heavens will pass away with a roar"**: Jesus already declared that "heaven and earth will pass away" (Mat. 24:35), although He offered no explanation at that time. Peter looks ahead to this "passing" of the physical universe; John "saw" beyond that "passing," when all that remained was the spiritual world in which the redeemed live forever with God and all the rest of human souls have been cast "outside" the city of God (Rev. 21:1, 8). To "pass away," as Peter uses the phrase, means to go away forever or to perish.[248] "Roar" [Greek, *rhoizos*] literally refers to the sound of an arrow whizzing by, the rush of wings, or the hissing of a serpent.[249] It seems that Peter simply means that it will produce a distinct and unmistakable sound, one that will clearly signal the end of all things (cf. 1 Cor. 15:52 and 1 Thess. 4:16).

❑ **"the elements will be destroyed with intense heat"**: "Elements" [Greek, *stoicheion*] literally refers to the primary building blocks, or rudimentary parts, of a much larger construction of something.

---

248 Strong, *Dictionary* (electronic), G3928.

249 Vincent, *Word Studies* (electronic), on 3:10.

For example, it is used to describe the letters of the alphabet, the basic components of knowledge (Col. 2:8), or the child–like, first principles of human understanding (Gal. 4:3, 9). It refers, then, to the smallest of things that cannot be reduced to anything smaller.[250] In the physical context, this refers to the irreducible components of the material world, whatever these are. But it can also have reference to the basic components of a larger system in another sense, as referring to the moon, planets, sun, and stars of our universe.[251] "Destroyed" [Greek, *luo*] can also be translated "melted," "dissolved," or "broken up."[252] The agent of this destruction will be fire ("intense heat") (recall 3:7).

❑ **"the earth and its works [or, the works in it] will be burned up":** Not only will the universe be completely destroyed, but so will the earth itself.[253] Many assume that, while societies change and technology changes how we function in society, the physical world and how it operates will go on indefinitely. It is difficult for us to imagine anything other than what we know now. We also do our best to preserve the monuments, relics, and documentation of human history, since we think that this serves to keep humanity alive and connected. Yet, Peter points us to a day in our future when there will be no more earth upon which to live, and therefore no more "works" of human achievement to remember. God will not have huge museums in heaven to preserve what we built, invented, wrote, painted, or accomplished here on earth; what He accomplishes through us—and especially through His Son—will be

---

250 *Ibid.,* on 3:10.

251 JFB, *Commentary* (electronic), on 3:10.

252 Strong, *Dictionary* (electronic), G3089.

253 Kistemaker translates this: "and the earth and everything in it will be laid bare," drawing on a variant reading of ancient NT manuscripts (*NTC,* 336–337). But the *context* of this passage is not about merely purging the earth of its works, but that the earth will be destroyed in the exact same manner and to the exact same degree as the heavens—i.e., destroyed with "intense heat" (3:12). When these two scenarios—the destruction of the heavens and the destruction of the earth—are made equal, the outcome must also be equal, not different. Just as we would never conclude that the *heavens* are going to be "laid bare," neither should we conclude that the *earth* will be laid bare. Rather, they *both* will be equally, simultaneously, and thoroughly destroyed.

all that matters. "Burned up" once again implies fire as the agent of destruction.[254]

Given what is sure to come, Peter exhorts his readers to live in such a way as to prepare for it (3:11). This is not a *plausible* situation ("Suppose all these things…"), but one that is *sure to happen* ("Since all these things…"). The exhortation is put in the form of a rhetorical question, as in, "What do you think should be your response to what I have told you?" "Holy conduct" here means pious behavior or reverent lifestyle (recall 1 Peter 1:13–16). "Godliness" refers to acting in a godly manner, as befits children of God (Eph. 5:1; see 1 Tim. 2:2, 6:11, Titus 1:1, 2 Peter 1:3, etc.). Not only is the "day of God" coming, but those who *are* living with holy conduct and godliness ought to be anticipating and even "hastening" it (3:12). "Hastening" means to urge on, to wait with eager anticipation and desire.[255] Instead of regarding the day of the Lord with dread and a "terrifying expectation of judgment" (Heb. 10:27), Christians should look forward to the time when God and His people will be united forever, and when God will bring about justice against the sinful world (Isa. 35:4, in principle).

Peter then reiterates his point that the heavens *will* be burned up and the elements (of the heavens, the earth, and every human work) *will* be melted "with intense heat." His reason for this repetition is to emphasize the surety, universality, and finality of what is coming. No one can claim exemption to it; no one can delay or prevent it from happening; therefore, *everyone* ought to prepare for it.

---

254 Barnes argues that there is no reason to believe that the physical world will be *annihilated* but will only be reduced to its smallest component or elements (*Barnes' Notes*, on 3:10). In my opinion, since *everything* in the material universe is energy in a certain form (a nod to Albert Einstein for proving this), God will simply reduce all material in the universe to pure energy. All energy that once came *from* God to produce the physical Creation will return *to* Him. If this is true, then it means that the entire universe will erupt in a cataclysmic explosion as all the energy in every atom is unleashed like a cosmic nuclear bomb, thus reducing *all* things to its smallest form— raw energy itself.

255 Strong, *Dictionary* (electronic), G4692.

This begs the question: if God is going to destroy the *present* heavens (cosmos) and earth—the dwelling place that God *once* created for us—then where will His people live? Peter answers: "we are looking for *new* heavens and a *new* earth" (3:13, emphases added). The ungodly cannot look forward to this, but only faithful Christians. "According to His promise" indicates that this is not a new idea but one that has already been stated. The closest we can find such an idea stated is in Isaiah:

❑ "For behold, I create new heavens and a new earth; and the former things will not be remembered or come to mind" (Isa. 65:17). (I recommend reading the fuller context: Isa. 65:8–25.)

❑ "'For just as the new heavens and the new earth which I make will endure before Me,' declares the LORD, 'so your offspring and your name will endure'" (Isa. 66:22). (Again, I recommend reading the fuller context: Isa. 66:10–24.)

In these celebrated yet often misunderstood or wrongly interpreted passages, it *appears* to support the Premillennialistic idea of a rejuvenated earth in which all natural dangers are removed, and all natural expectations will be changed ("weeping and the sound of crying" will be gone; "the wolf and the lamb will graze together"; etc.). Yet, Isaiah saw ahead to the *spiritual regeneration* of Israel, not a literal description of our physical world. Things in the kingdom of God will *not* follow the usual expectations (since "the first shall be last, and the last shall be first"; "whoever wishes to be great among you shall be your servant"; etc.); natural dangers and earthly troubles will *not* destroy God's people (see Mat. 10:28, Rom. 8:35–39, 2 Cor. 12:9–10, 1 Peter 3:13–14, etc.). Put another way: Isaiah prophesied about spiritual life in Christ's *church*, not our day–to–day existence on a refurbished earth. An objective study of Isaiah will bear this out.[256]

God is going to destroy the physical system, not merely overhaul it. The physical world—the creation of which is described in Gen. 1—serves several distinct purposes:

---

256 I recommend my *A Study of Isaiah* (Spiritbuilding Publishers, 2025); go to www. spiritbuilding.com/chad.

- a testament of God's power and authority (Rom. 1:20).
- a dwelling place for human beings; as a dominion over which men are to rule (Heb. 2:5–8).
- a time for all people to choose between God and anything else (Deut. 30:15–18, in principle).
- the coexistence of the righteous and the unrighteous.
- as a kind of cosmic theater stage for ushering in God's Son in the middle of time and all humanity, to demonstrate God's love and salvation to humankind.

Once these purposes have been fulfilled—to the extent that there is no longer any need for them, *and* nothing further will be gained by perpetuating the present system—God will call all of it to a close by destroying it completely. Once Christ's reign over God's kingdom has served *its* purpose—i.e., to provide for the redemption of men—then Christ will hand the kingdom back over to His Father and there will be no longer any opportunity for redemption (1 Cor. 15:22–28).

Everything God does moves things *forward*, never *backward*. There is no reason to believe that God will go *back* to an earthly Garden of Eden, but He will take His people *forward* to a spiritual Paradise in the heavenly realm. In the Garden of Eden, God walked with Adam and Eve in the world He had created for them; in the spiritual context, we walk with—and, if faithful, will live forever in—the presence of God in *His* world (Rev. 21:22–27, 22:1–5). God will not give us a reformatted dwelling place in which to live, but an entirely *new* one (Rev. 21:5). This present physical world lies under a divine curse (Gen. 3:16–19); whatever God has cursed is set apart for destruction, not renovation (John 15:6, in principle). The future spiritual existence of God's people, however, has no curse, or anything to remind them of a curse, or anything connected *with* a curse (Rom. 8:19–23, Rev. 22:3). God is not going to redeem the planet—He has *never* promised this—but He *will* redeem His people—*this* He has promised.

"In which righteousness dwells" (3:13b) means: this new dwelling place of God's people will not be a place (or state of being) in which godly and wicked people coexist, or where sin will be present. Rather, it will be an existence that is entirely consistent with the One who provided it, so that God's people will live securely in His righteousness, not afraid of enemies or assaulted with temptations to sin against Him. "I will be their God and they will be My people" is the persistent theme of the entire Bible, and when His people are finally with their God, they will dwell in righteousness forever.

Closing Remarks
(2 Peter 3:14–18)

Peter instructed his readers to eagerly anticipate the coming of the day of the Lord (recall 3:12). Now he implies that they have indeed been doing this, and thus believe all of what he has said (3:14). "Be diligent to be found *by Him* in peace …" (emphasis added)—the standard of measurement that Christians ought to use in determining where they stand with God must be Christ, not themselves or anything else (1 Cor. 4:3–4). When He comes, He will "find" us by seeing us as we are, since we cannot escape His omniscient detection. Diligence involves strenuous and continual effort (recall 1:5); one's presentation before God's tribunal is not something to be taken lightly. "Peace" is possible only through unity between God and the believer; His grace, through our faith, reconciles us with Him and removes our condemnation (Rom. 5:1–2, 8:1, 15:13, 2 Cor. 13:11, etc.). "Spotless [or, unstained] and blameless" indicates our innocence before God once we have been cleansed by the blood of Christ (Eph. 5:27, Phil. 2:15, Col. 1:19–22, 1 John 1:7, etc.)—the exact opposite of false teachers (recall 2:13).

We must not view God's patience as the lack of His ability or follow-through, as we have discussed earlier (in 3:3–9). Instead, we should look upon God's patience with us—and with the world—"as salvation" (3:15a). He is giving all of us time to repent, because He desires us to be *saved*, and that none should be lost (1 Tim. 1:15 and 2:4). Sinful people have no right to claim that, because God has not yet come, they can sin without accountability or punishment, or that God is not faithful in His promise *to* punish them. God will indeed punish the ungodly world but will *spare* all those who call upon Him for salvation. On the other hand, He will not wait forever, especially if the world becomes insensitive to His kindness and blessings (Rom. 2:4; see Rev. 2:20–22 as a small–scale example of this).

At this point in his epistle, Peter defers to the apostle Paul—for there can be no other "Paul" identified here—and his writings (3:15b–16a). Despite the two men's difficult experience years earlier (see Gal. 2:11–14), Peter speaks respectfully and supportively of Paul, regarding him as "our beloved brother." The "wisdom given" to Paul likely refers to his having been inspired by God through divinely revealed knowledge (Gal. 1:11–12). The fact that Paul "wrote to" the same people to whom Peter now writes indicates an overlapping of the two apostles' ministries, as well as an agreement between their teachings. Not only this, but by this time some of Paul's epistles had already been circulating throughout the brotherhood and may have been well known by the churches.

Peter does concede, however, that some of Paul's writings are "hard to understand" (3:16a). This gives *us* a bit of comfort since we continue to struggle with Paul's teachings to this day. This does not mean such things *cannot* be understood or were *purposely* made difficult to understand, but that it requires effort and study *to* understand them. "These things" implies that the subjects over which Christians wrestle in Paul's writings are some of the same in which Peter himself has addressed—e.g., the new birth, the serious duty of believers toward prayer and holy living, the Second Coming, the end of the physical system, the judgment to come, and the difficulty of being prepared for the world to come.

Struggling to understand something is one thing; distorting it is quite another (3:16b). "Distort" means to twist, wrench, wrest, or pervert; it once described the twisting or dislocating of the limbs of one being tortured.[257] The mangling of God's word in this case is intentional,

---

257 Strong, *Dictionary* (electronic), G4761; Vincent, *Word Studies* (electronic), on 3:16.

not the result of some simple misunderstanding. Those doing the mangling are the "untaught" and "unstable"—people opposed to the truth, being unwilling to receive it for what it is. Since they themselves are unstable and unsettled, their teachings are also this way; as they do with Paul's writings, so they do with "the rest of the Scriptures." Those who intentionally distort God's sacred word will be destroyed; those who refuse to listen to God's prophets bring upon themselves divine condemnation (Acts 3:22–23); and those who alter in any way God's written word are accursed (Rev. 22:18–19, by extension).

"You therefore, beloved, knowing this beforehand …" (3:17)—another way of saying: you have been warned, so there is no reason why you should be taken in by such false teaching. "Be on your guard" means be aware of what is going on and what is being taught; do not be gullible toward or accepting of everything you hear; and put to test that which you *do* hear (1 John 4:1, Rev. 2:2). Such a warning reminds us of that which Paul gave to the Ephesian elders (Acts 20:28–31): "be on guard for yourselves and for all the flock"; "be on the alert."

Christians have a moral responsibility to hold teachers and preachers of the gospel accountable; *they* (Christians) are the ones told to "be on your guard," not the preachers. The failure to be alert and discerning causes otherwise good men and women to be led astray by the "smooth and flattering speech" (Rom. 16:18) of deceivers. Just because people have been Christians for some time does not make them immune to slipping from their steadfastness or sure footing; "Therefore let him who thinks he stands take heed that he does not fall" (1 Cor. 10:12). (On "unprincipled men," see notes on 2:7.) False teachers are in the same condemned category as the sexually deviant men of Sodom and Gomorrah. Corrupting the revealed word of God is as criminal as corrupting the natural order of Creation.

Instead of *falling* as the result of being carried away from the truth, Peter strongly urges his readers to *grow* in the knowledge and grace of that truth (3:18a). God's divine truth is not something separate from Christ Himself, since "truth is in Jesus" (Eph. 4:21). Growing in godly knowledge—with the intention of drawing near to God Himself—necessarily requires a solid grasp of Christ's personal character, virtue, and ministry. It is impossible to draw near to God without first hearing the gospel of His Son, which includes knowing the *love* and *work* of His Son. Jesus Himself said, "I am the way, and the truth, and the life; no one comes to the Father but through Me" (John 14:6); and, "He who has seen Me has seen the Father" (John 14:9).

"Grace"—always referring to a gift of God—has different applications in the NT. It can refer to:

- God's benevolence toward all people (Mat. 5:45, in principle; Rom. 2:4), especially as demonstrated through Jesus Christ (John 1:17, 2 Cor. 8:9).
- God's message, the gospel, as revealed through divine revelation (Acts 14:3 and 20:32, "the word of His grace"; Acts 20:24, "the gospel of the grace of God"; Gal. 1:6; etc.).
- God's divine providence toward believers (1 Cor. 15:10, 2 Cor. 12:9), sometimes in the form of specific gifts, both miraculous (1 Cor. 12:4–7, gifts of grace, by implication) and otherwise (Rom. 12:6, Eph. 4:7, 1 Peter 4:11, etc.).
- God's *saving* grace, which is everything He does for believers that they cannot do for themselves regarding salvation (Rom. 3:24, 5:1–2, 1 Cor. 1:4, Eph. 2:8, etc.).

The question is: to which "grace" application does Peter here refer (3:18a)? In a sense, *all* of them, since Christians ought to be very interested in *every* form of God's kindness that is made available. But, in the context of Peter's other statements, the *gospel message* is the most natural conclusion. It is this (message) that the false teachers are perverting; it is this that Christians need to keep intact, not only for themselves but also for all whom they teach; and it is this that is most closely associated with "knowledge." The gospel message is *grace* because it was given to us as a gift by God; it is the sound doctrine of *saving* grace; and it is needed and beneficial, as are all of God's gifts (James 1:17). As such, this "grace" is something believers ought to actively pursue, and not take for granted or be ignorant of. The message of God's grace is the single most important one that exists on the earth for all time. Everything we know *factually* about God, His Son, the human soul, sin, salvation, and the afterlife is in that message.

"To Him be the glory" (3:18b)—the antecedent of "Him" being "our Lord and Savior Jesus Christ"—because He is "the summing up of all things" in heaven (God's world) and the earth (our world) (Eph. 1:10). Christ holds all things together, both in the spiritual world as well as the physical world (Col. 1:16–18). He has proven Himself to be worthy of all glory, praise, and worship, and therefore is deserving of these (as demonstrated in Rev. 5:11–14). He deserves such glory *now*—for who He is and what He has already done—and "to the day of eternity"—for who He will always be and what He will forever do for His people. Upon His Second Coming, Christ's church (His "bride") will be brought into heavenly splendor, in which He will share His glory, wealth, and dominion with all the redeemed. Thus, it is only fitting that those who *are* redeemed should worship Him as their eternal Lord and Savior.

Sources Used for *1 & 2 Peter*

Anderson, Dr. Lynn. *They Smell Like Sheep*, vol. 1. New York: Howard Books, 1997.

Barclay, William. *The Letters of James and Peter*. Philadelphia: Westminster Press, 1960.

Barnes, Albert. *Barnes' Notes on the New Testament* (electronic edition). Database © 2014 by WORDsearch Corp.

Butler, Trent C., gen. ed. *Holman's Illustrated Bible Dictionary* (electronic edition). © 2003 by Holman Bible Publishers; database © 2014 by WORDsearch Corp.

Caffin, B. C. "1 Peter," "2 Peter." *The Pulpit Commentary*, vol. 22. Peabody, MA: Hendrickson Publishers, no date.

Clowney, Edmund. *The Message of 1 Peter*. Downers Grove, IL: InterVarsity Press, 1988.

Cogdill, Roy E. *The New Testament: Book by Book*. Marion, IN: Cogdill Foundation Publication, 1975.

Dawson, Samuel G. *II Peter 3: Destruction of Universe or Destruction of Jerusalem?* Amarillo, TX: Gospel Themes Press, 1997 (pamphlet).

Foxe, John. *Foxe's Book of Martyrs*. Roanoke, VA: Scripture Truth, no date.

Green, Michael. *Tyndale New Testament Commentary: 2 Peter and Jude*. Grand Rapids: Wm. Eerdmans Publishing Co., 1987.

Jamieson, Robert; Andrew Fausset; David Brown. *Jamieson, Fausset, and Brown Commentary: Commentary Critical and Explanatory on the Whole Bible (1871)* (electronic edition). Database © 2012 by WORDsearch Corp.

Kistemaker, Simon J. *New Testament Commentary: Exposition of the Epistles of Peter and the Epistle of Jude*. Grand Rapids: Baker Book House, 1987.

Lenski, R. C. H. *Commentary on the New Testament: The Interpretation of the Epistles of St. Peter, St. John, and Jude.* Peabody, MA: Hendrickson Publishers, 1998.

Merriam-Webster's 11th Collegiate Dictionary (electronic edition). © 2003 by Merriam–Webster, Inc., v. 3.0.

Michaels, J. Ramsey. *Word Biblical Commentary, vol. 49: 1 Peter.* Waco, TX: Word Books, 1988.

Robertson, Archibald T. *Word Pictures in the New Testament,* electronic edition. © 1960 by The Sunday School Board of the Southern Baptist Convention; database © 2007 by WORDsearch Corp.

Stibbs, Alan M. *Tyndale New Testament Commentary: The First General Epistle of Peter.* Grand Rapids: Wm. B. Eerdmans Publishing Co., 1983.

Stoop, J. Ridley, ed. *Restoration Ideas on Church Organization.* Nashville: David Lipscomb College, no date.

Strong, James. *Strong's Talking Greek–Hebrew Dictionary* (electronic edition). Database © WORDsearch Corp.

Sychtysz, Chad. *1 & 2 Timothy Commentary.* Waynesville, OH: Spiritbuilding Publishers, 2024.

_____. *1–2–3 John and Jude Commentary.* Waynesville, OH: Spiritbuilding Publishers, 2024.

_____. *Titus and James Commentary.* Waynesville, OH: Spiritbuilding Publishers, 2024.

The International Standard Bible Encyclopedia (electronic edition). © 1979 by Wm. B. Eerdmans Publishing Co.; database © 2013 by WORDsearch Corp.

Thomas, Robert L., and W. Don Wilkins, gen. eds. *New American Standard Hebrew, Aramaic, and Greek Dictionary* (electronic edition). © 1981, 1998 by the Lockman Foundation.

Vincent, Marvin R. *Vincent's Word Studies,* vol 1 (electronic edition). Database © 2014 by WORDsearch Corp.

Welch, Edward J. *Addictions: A Banquet in the Grave.* Phillipsburg, NJ: P & R Publishing Co., 2001.

Woods, Guy N. *A Commentary on the New Testament Epistles of Peter, John, and Jude.* Nashville: Gospel Advocate Co., 1979.

www.ingramcontent.com/pod-product-compliance
Lightning Source LLC
Chambersburg PA
CBHW050818090426
42737CB00021B/3424